Pastors *and* Elders

CARING FOR THE CHURCH AND ONE ANOTHER

Timothy J. Mech

CONCORDIA PUBLISHING HOUSE · SAINT LOUIS

Copyright © 2011 Concordia Publishing House
3558 S. Jefferson Ave., St. Louis, MO 63118-3968
1-800-325-3040 • www.cph.org

Library of Congress Cataloging-in-Publication Data

Mech, Timothy J.
  Pastors and elders : caring for the church and one another / Timothy J. Mech.
    p. cm.
  ISBN 978-0-7586-2747-6
  1. Clergy--Office. 2. Elders (Church officers) 3. Christian leadership. I. Title.
  BV660.3.M43 2011
  253--dc23

                              2011042216

---

 2 3 4 5 6 7 8 9 10   20 19 18 17 16 15

CONTENTS

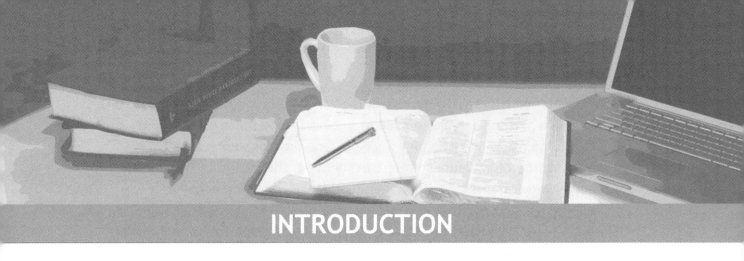

INTRODUCTION

A resource was needed to assist pastors and elders in caring for the Church and one another. While at first reluctant to take on such a task, the current state of many relationships between pastors and elders and their congregations led me to recognize the great need for such a resource. On the one hand, I have observed pastors become so frustrated with their elders and congregations that they have contemplated pursuing another vocation or have actually resigned. Others have been forced out. On the other hand, pastors who refuse to be held accountable to the congregational leadership have intimidated many elders. This has led, in some cases, to people leaving their home congregation or even the Church. Other issues include elders simply not knowing what to do or not having the tools to carry out the task of assisting the pastor in caring for the congregation. In addition, strengths and weaknesses of pastors and elders have not been identified so that in some areas of ministry the pastor or elder has been set up to fail. Instead of using the gifts of a person's particular vocation, the pastor or elder has been asked to do something that he is not trained or comfortable doing. On top of that, both pastors and elders are given the very difficult task of addressing members of the congregation, who are bombarded by and submerged into a self-absorbed culture. Pastors and elders are at times perceived as barriers to people doing and getting what they want. A pastor or elder call on a member of a congregation is often not welcomed by parishioners, especially those who are inactive or who are involved in something contrary to the Word of God.

I've been a Lutheran pastor for the past twenty-one years. My first call was to a small congregation with an average Sunday attendance of around forty-five people. I currently serve a large congregation of over 1,600 members with a school (3-year-olds through eighth grade) of 155 students. I've worked with elders on issues as diverse as helping a struggling congregation survive a scandal to personnel issues that led to a church worker being removed from office through a voter's assembly. Successful resolutions were reached in both cases because of a relationship of trust between the pastor and elders. The church worker remains a faithful member of the congregation, and my previous congregation not only survives but continues to thrive on the Gospel of Jesus Christ. Through these experiences and others, I've learned the value of a trusting and respectful relationship with elders. Through the years we have encouraged, taught, admonished, confided in, and forgiven one another. The positive relationships that I have had with elders were one of the reasons I was asked to write this book.

Pastors and Elders will address the issues of who is in charge in the Church, what elders do, trust between elders and pastors, dealing with a self-absorbed culture, working within one's vocation, and how pastors and elders can hold one another accountable to God. This book is also intended to be used as a training guide in the monthly board of elders meetings. Discussion questions at the end of each chapter, along with the videos found on the enhanced DVD (CPH 15-5177), will give opportunity to work through the issues identified in each chapter. My prayer is that this resource will assist pastors and elders in faithfully caring for the Church and for one another.

WHO'S IN CHARGE?

Chapter ONE

Jesus [said], "All authority in heaven and
on earth has been given to Me."

—Matthew 28:18

A member of the board of elders expresses a concern. His pastor says, "Your job is to keep your ears open and your mouth shut." A pastor adheres to a particular scriptural practice. One of his elders insists that the church take a survey to determine whether the congregation wants to eliminate this unpopular practice. Both responses are attempts to dictate and control what goes on in the church; they are an effort to grab power for oneself at the expense of others.

But does having more power in the church solve problems or create them? The above scenarios highlight the fact that the source of many problems within the church, especially problems between pastors and elders, is confusion between spiritual authority and power. Rev. John W. Kleinig, who has spoken extensively on this topic, talks about the difference between power and authority.

> Power is a limited ability or commodity. A person has power at the expense of someone else. I must disempower others in order to have it and keep it for myself. Those who lack authority use power. When people operate with power the reaction to them is political. If you operate with power than you have a constant battle with the other power people in your congregation. That leads you to manipulation by the great power-monger, Satan. Operate with power and you are operating on Satan's terms.

> Authority is an unlimited ability or commodity. You cannot ex-

What is the difference between power and authority

Talk about my teaching discipline in the class.

(handwritten: power is taken)

ercise authority unless you are under authority. It is never taken. Authority is given to you by someone else. You can only receive it. I exercise authority by authorizing others to act. You don't exercise authority by keeping it to yourself. The more I give my authority away the greater my authority is. Authority grows with the delegation of authority to others. When authorities speak people listen, even if they don't agree.[1]

(handwritten: allow my students to have say on how my class is run)

The answer for problems in the church, then, is not to have more power, but to exercise proper authority. Jesus said, "All authority in heaven and on earth has been given to Me" (Matthew 28:18). The source of all authority in the Church is Jesus, not the pastor or elder or other members of the congregation. Jesus is in charge, and He authorizes His people to serve in His Church through various vocations.

The apostle Peter writes of all Christians, "But you are a chosen race, a royal priesthood, a holy nation, a people for His own possession, that you may proclaim the excellencies of Him who called you out of darkness into His marvelous light. . . . Live as people who are free, not using your freedom as a cover-up for evil, but living as servants of God" (1 Peter 2:9, 16). Elders, as members of the priesthood of all believers, are authorized to be servants in the Church.

Strictly speaking, the word "elder" in the Bible (Acts 14:23; 1 Tim. 5:17–19, Titus 1:5–9 and 1 Peter 5:1–4) refers to those who hold the pastoral office. What we commonly call "elders" today are laymen appointed to serve the congregation in its temporal affairs and to assist the pastor in administrative tasks. . . . Later such men came to be known as the "deacons" (meaning "servants"). As you can see, Scripture does not define the exact role of such deacons, only their qualifications (1 Timothy 3:8–13). Scripture gives them no special spiritual responsibilities in the congregation beyond those given to every Christian.

(handwritten: Elders refer to the regal priesthood) (Interesting)

While the office of pastor is divinely instituted and indispensable for the Church, the deacon is an optional office based on apostolic and church custom.

The deacon or elder is a position of lay-service, concerned with the temporal and administrative affairs of the congregation. In many congregations deacons or elders are also charged with oversight of the pastor. But, rightly understood according to Scripture, they exercise only that oversight given to every Christian in the congregation.[2]

that is true for all members of the Church

Pastors ordained into the Office of the Public Ministry are authorized by God through the Church to preach the Word of God and administer the Sacraments according to the Word of God. The apostle Paul writes, "I charge you in the presence of God and of Christ Jesus, who is to judge the living and the dead, and by His appearing and His kingdom; preach the word; be ready in season and out of season; reprove, rebuke, and exhort, with complete patience and teaching" (2 Timothy 4:1–2). Jesus said of one in this office, "The one who hears you hears Me, and the one who rejects you rejects Me, and the one who rejects Me rejects the one who sent Me" (Luke 10:16).

Pastors are servants of Christ.

Concerning this office [of the Public Ministry] we teach that it is a divine ordinance; that is, the Christians of a certain locality must apply the means of grace not only privately and within the circle of their families nor merely in their common intercourse with fellow-Christians, John 5:39; Eph. 6:4; Col. 3:16, but they are also required, by the divine order, to make provision that the Word of God be publicly preached in their midst, and the sacraments administered according to the institution of Christ, by persons qualified for such work, whose qualifications and official functions are exactly defined in Scripture, Titus 1:5; Acts 14:23; 20:28; 2 Tim. 2:2.

Although the office of the ministry is a divine ordinance, it possesses no other power than the power of the Word of God, 1 Pet. 4:11; that is to say, it is the duty of Christians to yield unconditional obedience to the office of the ministry whenever, and as long as, the minister proclaims to them the Word of God, Heb. 13:17, Luke 10:16. If, however, the minister, in his teachings and injunctions, were to go beyond the Word of God, it would be the duty of Christians not to obey, but to disobey him, so as to

Listen and obey Pastor if he adheres to the Word

remain faithful to Christ, Matt. 23:8. Accordingly, we reject the false doctrine ascribing to the office of the ministry the right to demand obedience and submission in matters which Christ has not commanded.[3]

At his ordination, a pastor is given orders to be under authority; to say what the Lord says through this Office of the Public Ministry. The pastor in turn vows to humbly accept this yoke, promising to faithfully preach and teach the Word of God. The robe and stole a pastor wears in the Divine Service beautifully illustrate the terms of his office: who the pastor represents, the extent of his authority, and what he is given to say. The robe covers the man and declares that the words he speaks are not his own. The stole, placed as a yoke around his neck, represents the vow the pastor made to faithfully preach and teach the Word of God.

The robe and stole worn by the pastor teach this even to little children. A little girl who was new to the congregation said to her friend in the pew, "See that guy in the black shirt? That's the pastor. When he puts his dress, on he's Jesus."

Notice the understanding that when the pastor puts on the robe and stole, he represents someone else, namely, Jesus. When faithfully preaching and teaching the Word of God, it could be said by any pastor, "If you don't like what I have to say, see the Lord about it. I only work here!" But it is important to highlight the fact that the pastor, in his official capacity, is authorized to say what Jesus says, nothing more and nothing less. This means that in other church matters, it would be wrong for the pastor to try to use power to get people to do what he cannot otherwise do solely on the basis of his authority. For example, saying that God wants the congregation to begin a building project or pass a particular budget would be a misuse of the pastor's authority.

Doctors who made house calls often carried a medical bag that included a number of instruments, each designed to help the doctor diagnose and cure the patient's pain and ailment. As the doctor would pull the needed instrument from the bag, it sent a subtle, but authoritative message: *the doctor is at work*. The doctor is at work, and healing is on its way.

[handwritten margin notes: "They should look at him first as Jesus talking to them" and "Can't go beyond his authority"]

The pastor has instruments that he is authorized to use for the care and cure of souls, namely, the Lord's Word and Sacraments. The Word of God consists of both Law and Gospel. Like the stethoscope used by a doctor, the Law's main purpose is to listen inside and identify what is wrong with us. In other words, the main purpose of the Law is to show us our sin. The Law is not an end in and of itself. It serves the Gospel just as a doctor's diagnosis of a medical problem serves the process of healing. When our sin is brought to light, that is, confessed, it is identified and there is a desire for the sin to be removed.

The purpose of the Gospel is to forgive our sin, to remove it from our very being. This is done through the Absolution, the declarative word of the Lord's forgiveness. Just as a stethoscope is an invaluable instrument in a doctor's medical bag, one of the most important tools in the pastor's "spiritual medical bag" is private Confession and Absolution. The pastors asks the penitent, "Do you believe that my forgiveness is God's forgiveness?" With the acknowledgement that it is, indeed, God's forgiveness being bestowed, the pastor places his hands on the head of the penitent and says, "In the stead and by the command of my Lord Jesus Christ I forgive you all your sins in the name of the Father and of the Son and of the Holy Spirit" (*LSB*, p. 293). In Confession and Absolution, the source of our pain and agony, namely sin, is healed by the authority of Jesus Christ.

There is also a miracle medicine of immortality found within the pastor's spiritual medical bag. It is called the Lord's Supper, the very body and blood of Jesus Christ. Through Christ's authority, the pastor puts these into the mouth, heart, and life of penitents for the forgiveness of sins, that believing, they might rejoice in what God has given and respond with thanksgiving.

An example of someone who believed and rejoiced in God's gifts given through the Lord's Supper was a woman by the name of Bev. Bev and her mother were shut-ins, confined to their home due to illness. Bev knew that there was more going on than met the eye when the pastor, acting under Christ's authority, served the Lord's Supper to her and her mother. It is why she wanted the pastor of her church to have a Communion set that confessed the importance of what was being served even there, namely, the Lord's very body and blood, given and shed for the forgiveness of their sins.

So one year during Lent Bev gave up her phone, setting aside the money she saved. And that Easter, this woman on a fixed income gave her pastor a new communion set, complete with a beautiful silver plate and chalice. What a beautiful response to what God had given! What a beautiful confession of the authority of God's Word! Bev felt, "Since the Lord's forgiveness is given through His body and blood in Communion, the vessels that deliver these gifts should make a statement about their importance." The pastor will be using this Communion set for his entire ministry, not only because of the silver plate and chalice, but because of the wonderful confession of faith that led to the set being given for the distribution of the Lord's very body and blood to sinners needing forgiveness. Word and Sacraments—these are the instruments the pastor is authorized to use for the care and cure of souls.

a good wine

confession of faith

While great blessings come by acting in accord with the authority of God's Word, many problems occur within the congregation when a pastor or elder does something that he is not authorized to do. A pastor steps beyond his authority and purchases something that has not been budgeted for or approved by the congregation. An elder disregards the pastor's mandate to preach both Law and Gospel and promises a member that he will see to it that the pastor performs the marriage of the member's daughter who is living together with her boyfriend. An elder demands the pastor give the body and blood of Christ to a visitor who is a member of a church body that rejects the real presence of the Lord's body and blood in the Sacrament. These are examples of a pastor or elder exercising power instead of acting under the authority of his office with his given responsibilities.

making a pastor do something not according to the word.

When the board of elders or the pastor exercise power instead of authority, elders' meetings can quickly deteriorate into simply reacting to or complaining about the challenges and problems within a congregation, such as poor attendance, a lack of volunteers, or the shortcomings of the pastor(s) or elders. Meetings such as this often end in frustration with little or nothing being accomplished except ill will among those involved. The problem is that such meetings begin in the wrong place. Instead of beginning with God and His Word to address the issue of poor attendance, for example, these meetings typically assume that the pastor or congregation must be doing something wrong if people are not coming to church in large numbers.

power leads to blaming others for problems in the church

The reason for this presupposition is that we live in a consumerist culture. In marketing, the goal is to find out what consumers want and sell it to them. In such a system, the customer is always right. This is why many conclude that, in order to solve attendance problems, we need to ask members or others what it will take to get them to attend or to return to church. Members of the church, inactive members, and maybe even unbelievers are then given power within the church, even at the expense of God's Word. What is often not considered is that some people may not be attending church because they fail to recognize the need for Jesus Christ and His Word in their lives. They may have put other things ahead of God and His Word and thus trust in someone or something other than Jesus Christ. Instead of consulting them as to what the congregation should do, we need to speak the authoritative Word of God to them.

Ask others what will make you attend more often

to members not coming

In such cases, both pastor(s) and elders need to trust in the authority of God's Word to bring people to repentance and faith through the Gospel of Jesus Christ. It may take longer to turn things around, but the results are eternal. Dietrich Bonhoeffer writes that we do not build the Church, but Christ builds the Church by the authority of His Word.

Find ways to have God's word readed to others

We shall confess—he shall build. We shall preach—he shall build. We shall pray to him—he shall build. We do not know his plan. We do not see whether he builds or tears down. It may be that the times, which by human standards are times of collapse, are for him the times of great building. It may be that the times, which by human standards are times of great success, are for him the times to tear down. It is a great comfort that Christ gives to his church: confess, preach, and bear witness to me. I alone will build as it pleases me. Don't give me orders. Do your job—then you have done enough. You are all right. Don't seek out reasons and opinions. Don't keep judging. Don't keep checking again and again to see if you are secure. Church, remain a church! But, you, church—confess, confess, confess! You have only one Lord— Christ alone. By his grace alone you live. Christ builds.[4]

God does the building and tearing down

Great success by human standards may lead to God tearing down

Holy Spirit goes as he wishes!

We keep preaching

There are all sorts of things that pastors and elders may have the power to do, but it is only those things done by the authority of Jesus Christ that will stand the test of time. His words are different than ours because they have authority. Take note of what Jesus' words do. Jesus "rebuked the wind and said to the sea, 'Peace! Be still!' And the wind ceased, and there was great calm" (Mark 4:39). Jesus said to Lazarus who had been dead for four days, "Lazarus, come out" (John 11:43b). Lazarus came out of the tomb alive and well. Jesus said to the disciples in the Upper Room, " 'Peace be with you. As the Father has sent Me, even so I am sending you.' And when He had said this, He breathed on them and said to them, 'Receive the Holy Spirit. If you forgive the sins of anyone they are forgiven; if you withhold forgiveness from any, it is withheld' " (John 20:21–23). Jesus authorized His disciples to speak His words, words that deliver the forgiveness of sins. Jesus made them His apostles, that is, "sent ones," as He authorized them to deliver His life and salvation through the proclamation of the Gospel. It is the same with those in apostolic ministry today. Whether they come from Jesus' own lips, or out of the mouth of an apostle or pastor, people recognize that Jesus' words are different. They give and bestow what they say.

As an experienced pastor looked back at how he had conducted himself as a pastor, he recognized that it was when he operated according to the authority of his office that he had been most successful, as opposed to when he tried to get things done just because he had the power to do them. For example, in his first congregation the practice of offering the Lord's Supper every Sunday was not the accepted practice. Instead of declaring that he would immediately begin offering the Lord's Supper every Sunday, he patiently taught that, according to Scripture and our church body, weekly Communion would be a better congregational practice rather than celebrating it only on the first and third Sundays.

After a few years of patient teaching, he asked the congregation if they might add the fifth Sunday to the first and third as Communion Sundays. A member of the congregation said, "Pastor, you have taught that the best practice according to Scripture would be to offer the Lord's Supper every Sunday. Would it be all right if I offer a resolution that our congregation offer the Lord's Supper every Sunday?" It passed by unanimous vote. God's authoritative Word had done its work!

Later this same pastor observed other pastors trying to force this practice of weekly communion on their congregations. It turned out badly for all of them. In one case, the pastor was forced out of office. In the realm of power, there is always someone who has more of it than you.

At times, elders or other members in a congregation threaten that they are going to transfer to another church if the pastor either doesn't do something they like or stop doing something they don't like. This use of power by members or elders to get what they want can be demoralizing to a pastor. It puts enormous pressure on him, especially if those making these demands

[Handwritten margin notes: "Always someone that someone has more power than you." "Members may threaten to Leave." "Do we have members that have or try to use power?"]

Operating in the realm of power by doing things yourself seems easier than going through all the trouble of seeking the will of God in a certain situation, patiently teaching why something should be done, assisting someone in carrying out their vocation in the Church, or understanding the concerns of a person whose view is different than yours. There have been many times in ministry that pastors have carried out tasks that were properly given to congregational members to do simply because it was easier than equipping congregation members to do it. Many pastors still struggle with that. Pastors justify doing these things by concluding that if they don't do them, they won't get done. Truthfully, there *are* times that if the pastor doesn't complete the task it won't get done. However, failing to authorize and equip others for work in the congregation is a recipe for disaster. It robs the people of God the privilege and honor of serving the Lord in His Church. It takes the pastor away from the noble task of delivering the Lord's gifts of forgiveness, life, and peace to God's people. Sooner or later, the pastor will be crushed by the weight of trying to do everything himself. Worse, he may begin to think that he is indispensable or come to resent the people he serves because they don't do what he would like them to do.

are very influential in the congregation. The temptation is to give in to such ultimatums out of fear that if these people leave, it will destroy the congregation and the pastor's ministry. While acquiescing may seem to make things better for awhile, reacting to demands that are based on personal preference brings both pastor and people into the realm of political power and out of the realm of spiritual authority. We end up listening and following those with the most power instead of Jesus Christ who died for us, rose from the dead, and lives to serve us by the authority of His Word.

Pastors and elders need to continually ask themselves whether they are acting according to the authority of God's Word or something else when making decisions or condoning certain practices within the church. In our contemporary society, the authority for many is the power of one's feelings. Truth is often determined merely by one's subjective feelings, even when those feelings contradict objective reality. A member of a congregation said this to her pastor about what she believed, "Pastor, I don't care if it's not true, what matters is that it makes me feel good."

Feels good is good :-)

It is important to understand that even though feelings are real, they can be influenced or even manipulated by information that is false. For example, imagine that you drop your wife off at the airport for a work conference. As you drive home, you hear on the radio that the flight on which she was booked has crashed on takeoff and there are no survivors. How do you feel? You, of course, are crushed by sorrow and grief. Later on, however, you get a phone call from your wife letting you know that she took an earlier flight and is just fine. Now how do you feel? You are ecstatic! In both cases the feelings were real. The difference is that one set of feelings was based on false information while the other set of feelings was based on the truth.

Gossip gives false feelings

Never make decisions based on feelings

While the feelings of the pastor, elders, and other members of a congregation are important, decisions in the church are not to be made by the power of one's feelings. Instead, they are to be made by the authority of God's Word. Remember, Jesus is in charge. His Word gives and bestows what it says. Rev. Eugene Peterson writes that this is precisely why it is important for elders to hold pastors to their ordination vow to remain true to God's Word: the people need the stabilizing authority of the Word in the midst of influences bent on diluting or destroying faith. Instead of demanding their own way, elders, whether individually or as a group, should confess to their pastor that they have a need, and what that need is, according to the Word of God. Pastor Peterson expresses it this way:

> We need help in keeping our beliefs sharp and accurate and intact. We don't trust ourselves; our emotions seduce us into infidelities. We know we are launched on a difficult and dangerous act of faith, and there are strong influences intent on diluting or destroying it. We want you to give us help. Be our pastor, a minister of Word and sacrament in the middle of this world's life. . . .

> We are going to ordain you to this ministry, and we want your

vow that you will stick to it. This is not a temporary job assignment but a way of life that we need lived out in our community. We know you are launched on the same difficult belief venture in the same dangerous world as we are. We know your emotions are as fickle as ours, and your mind is as tricky as ours. That is why we are going to *ordain* you and why we are going to exact a *vow* from you. We know there will be days and months, maybe even years, when we won't feel like believing anything and won't want to hear it from you. And we know there will be days and weeks and maybe even years when you won't feel like saying it. It doesn't matter. Do it. You are ordained to this ministry, vowed to it. . . .

You are not the minister of our changing desires, or our time-conditioned understanding of our needs, or our secularized hopes for something better. With these vows of ordination we are lashing you fast to the mast of Word and sacrament so you will be unable to respond to the siren voices. . . .

Your task is to keep telling the basic story, representing the presence of the Spirit, insisting on the priority of God, speaking the biblical words of command and promise and invitation.[5]

As you think about the authority of the Lord's Word, think of a woman named Hilde. Hilde faithfully attended church and Bible class every week all her life. But eventually, Hilde was near death and being cared for in the home of her family. On one of her pastor's last visits to her, she was dressed in a beautiful white blouse with a gold cross necklace. She was lying in her granddaughter's bed and family members filled the room. She smiled and whispered into his ear, "Pastor, I'm not afraid. I'm ready to go home." How could Hilde have such confidence?

It was because she believed in the authority of the Word of God. Hilde believed Jesus when He said, "I am the resurrection and the life. Whoever believes in Me, though he die, yet shall he live, and everyone who lives and believes in Me shall never die" (John 11:25–26). She understood that God Himself is present with His gifts of salvation whenever and wherever we gather in the Lord's name to hear God's Word. She believed the Lord, who said,

[handwritten marginal note: What we really need to believe is that Jesus is our savior]

"For where two or three are gathered in My name, there am I among them" (Matthew 18:20).

How comforting for her family to witness her eager readiness to meet her Lord and Savior and to be reunited with her loved ones who had passed through death to life before her! Jesus said, "Peace be with you," and Hilde had peace. Jesus said, "Because I live, you also will live" (John 14:19), and Hilde now lives in the eternal glory of God.

Such is the authority that has been given by God the Father to our Lord Jesus Christ. Pastors are authorized to speak these words so that, as Jesus says, "My sheep hear My voice" (John 10:27a). By the authority of His Word, our Lord is still doing great things: "But that you may know that the Son of Man has authority on earth to forgive sins . . . [Jesus] said to the paralytic—'Rise, pick up your bed and go home.' And he rose and went home" (Matthew 9:6–7). By that same authority, Hilde and all believers in Christ head on home to heaven.

For Reflection and Discussion

1. What is the difference between spiritual authority and power?
2. How does Jesus exercise His authority in the church?
3. What are elders authorized to do in the congregation?
4. What is a pastor authorized to do in a congregation?
5. Why is it important to authorize others to work within the church?
6. What is the meaning of the robe and stole a pastor wears for the Divine Service?
7. What are the instruments a pastor is authorized to use for the care and cure of souls?
8. What problems may develop if a pastor or elder does something that he is not authorized to do?
9. What should a pastor and board of elders do before changing a certain practice within the church? Why?

10. Why is it dangerous to make decisions within the congregation on the basis of people's feelings?

11. Review the vows your pastor made at his ordination. Have you ever knowingly or unknowingly asked your pastor to do something that would violate his ordination vows?

ELDERS AT WORK

Chapter TWO

We ask you brothers, to respect those who labor among you and are over you in the Lord and admonish you, and to esteem them very highly in love because of their work. Be at peace among yourselves. And we urge you, brothers, admonish the idle, encourage the fainthearted, help the weak, be patient with them all. See that no one repays anyone evil for evil, but always seek to do good to one another and to everyone. Rejoice always, pray without ceasing, give thanks in all circumstances; for this is the will of God in Christ Jesus for you.

—1 Thessalonians 5:12–18

Herman was always the first one to church on Sunday mornings. He would often arrive even before the pastor and would wait for him to open the front door. He then went into the sanctuary and quietly prayed until the 8 a.m. service began. In addition, Herman sent his pastor notes from time to time thanking him for his sermons, encouraging him in his work as a pastor, and letting him know that he was always in his prayers. He respected and esteemed him highly in love because of his work as a pastor. Herman did that for all the pastors who served him throughout his life. Herman epitomized what servants in the church, including elders, are all about. They respect those authorized by our Lord through the church to deliver His gifts, and they seek to serve the Lord by speaking the truth in love and doing good to all.

Too often what we do in the Church is influenced or even directed by the word of a fallen humanity instead of the Word of the Lord. If the Word of God is not a part of the daily diet of both elders and pastors, the way of the congregation will begin to look more and more like the way of a fallen world. When this is the case, there is anger at the mere thought that elders of a congregation would, for example, be expected to attend a Bible class. A member of a congregation even said that he resigned from the board of elders and transferred to another congregation because the pastor required that all elders attend a Bible class. It is amazing how many people agreed with this person that going to a weekly Bible class was an unrealistic expectation of an elder. Many have disconnected the Word of God from their everyday lives, including elders, and yes, even some pastors. Among laity, many see the Word of God as simply important information to be taught instead of the very means by which God is active in our lives. Jesus said, "The words I have spoken to you are spirit and life" (John 6:63b), and "If you abide in Me, and My words abide in you, ask whatever you wish, and it will be done for you" (John 15:7). All members, especially elders, are encouraged to engage in the daily hearing or reading of the Word of God and in daily prayer for those entrusted to their care, and for all those in need.

Elders are given much to do in the church, but the most important work of elders takes place in their devotional lives. They need to be in the Word daily so that their lives are shaped and formed by the Word of God instead of the siren voices of a fallen world. A tool some churches use to assist the devotional lives of members is called the Green Sheet. The Green Sheet includes an order for daily devotions that includes a list of daily Scripture readings and the names of those in need of our prayers. The Green Sheet may also include the Introit of the Day, Collect, Gradual, the Scripture readings for the following Sunday, the Readings of the Day, a quote from a Church Father, a summary of the readings of the day, an explanation of the liturgy and hymns, and even a paragraph about the sermon (see Appendix A). The Green Sheet assists elders and other members of the church in carrying out their work as members of the priesthood of all believers as they take it home with them each week to use for their personal devotions.

Not everyone is qualified to be an elder within the church. It is important for congregations to look to Scripture and, on that basis, prayerfully consider the qualifications of those asked to serve as elders in the church. Rev. Victor A. Constien does just that when he writes of desirable qualities in elders for the congregation:

"As children of God through faith in Jesus, their Savior, elders

1. show a willingness to learn and grow in God's grace and the skills of serving Him and others;

2. demonstrate a faith which has been tested and refined through years of Christian experience;

3. faithfully participate in services of worship, the Lord's Supper, and small group adult Bible studies on Sunday and throughout the week;

4. pray regularly for the congregation, for its pastor and members, for their community, for all people, and for themselves;

5. lovingly work with their wives, if married, to strengthen their marriage and manage their households to fulfill God's purposes;

6. live personal lives which are above reproach;

7. exhibit mental and emotional stability;

8. demonstrate the ability to cultivate good interpersonal relationships, help people work toward solving personal problems, and live in love with those with whom they frequently clash;

9. show a deep commitment to the success of the congregation and the pastor as measured by God's goals for them;

10. exhibit a willingness to risk for the sake of Christ and His Gospel and to forgive when frail Christians are unable to carry out all their plans perfectly."[1]

The specific tasks of elders vary from congregation to congregation. Generally speaking, elders are to assist the pastor(s) in overseeing the spiritual life of the congregation and its individual members. Areas of responsibility include but are not limited to the following discussed below.

DIVINE SERVICES

Elders are authorized to

☐ oversee all services, making sure that they are held regularly, on time, and conducted decently and in order;

- provide an usher team at all services;

- maintain a welcoming atmosphere in the church before, during, and after all services;

- welcome all visitors and have them sign the guest or friendship register;

- be faithful in attending the weekly Divine Services, Advent, Lent, and Holy Week services;

- assist in providing the pastor(s) with adequate pulpit and altar assistance;

- keep accurate attendance records at all services;

- look for visitors at services, speak to them, and introduce them to others, including the pastor(s).

Offering assistance at the Divine Service is an important work of elders. For visitors, it can be very intimidating entering a sanctuary for the first time. Often, they will not sign the guest book or friendship register because they are checking things out. First impressions are important!

Elders should assist the pastor in making sure everyone feels welcome. One pastor, whenever he has the opportunity, walks around the sanctuary before the service to welcome people to the congregation. His elders are also charged with welcoming everyone entering the church. After one young couple that had been visiting became members, this pastor asked what it was that made them decide to join his congregation. They said he had them the moment he came by and introduced himself to them and welcomed them to the church. They also said that they had visited many congregations and at most of them no one bothered even to say hello. When pastors and elders are making an intentional effort to welcome everyone to church, it creates a friendly atmosphere. Demonstrating friendliness has a ripple effect and often results in other members of the congregation following that lead by welcoming those around them.

Care of the Pastor(s)

Elders are authorized to:

- "Serve as special assistants to the pastor(s), supporting them with prayer, helping them with special problems in his ministry; and concerning itself with the spiritual, emotional and physical health and welfare of the pastor(s) and their families. It shall ensure that they are provided with adequate compensation, housing and assistance with their work to guarantee them sufficient free time for personal responsibilities, study and relaxation." (See Appendix E.)

- Support the pastor in supervising the doctrine and practice of the congregation based on the Scriptures and the Lutheran Confessions.

- Take time to listen to the pastor's concerns in order to understand and assist him with problems or difficulties within the congregation.

- "Watch over the doctrine and life of the pastor without being watchdogs poised to pounce on him, and without feeling or showing distrust in the pastor's character and abilities. Help him in a spirit of brotherly love and harmony to feed and care for his flock with the pure Word, to maintain the practices of the church, and to set a proper example for the sheep and the lambs. Where pastoral abuses are evident, deal with them sensibly, employing words of admonition spoken in private and breathing patience, kindness, love and understanding. The intent cannot be to destroy the pastor but to treat him with utmost respect, gentleness and love—both as a pastor and Christian brother. The intent must be to assist the pastor to see his mistakes, to confess his sins and make amends, thus to win him from his error and restore him as a good, faithful and honorable shepherd of the flock. Only if such assistance and admonition is fruitless should the matter be taken to the Circuit Pastor."[2]

Who cares for pastors? Elders need to take the lead here. One area needing attention is the pastor getting time off from work. Pastors generally have the freedom to set their own schedules, but this can be both a curse and a blessing. It can be a curse if the pastor isn't good at scheduling himself in such a way that he is able to accomplish what he is given to do in the congregation. It can also be a curse due to the fact that the pastor's work is never done, and what he is given to do may change at any time of the day or night. This can lead to the pastor not taking the time off he needs to be refreshed and renewed and to fulfill his other vocations, such as his work as a husband, father, and friend. It can be a blessing in that he can choose his own day off, or, if need be, get away when he needs to by changing his schedule accordingly. Elders need to remember, however, that whenever the pastor takes time off, the work is still going to be there when he gets back. For example, there are still sermons and Bible studies to be prepared, visits to be made, and on-going pastoral care issues to attend to among members. Contrary to popular belief, most pastors do work more than just an hour on Sunday morning!

Some pastors are not efficient in keeping track of appointments or planning to ensure that things get done. These types of things can be corrected fairly easily with some assistance. Addressing issues such as this requires a genuine trust to be developed between pastors and elders. This trust allows for elders to feel free in giving constructive criticism and the pastor in feeling free to receive the help needed. Sadly, when trust is lacking, elders offer advice that is critical rather than constructive, and the pastor becomes defensive rather than receptive.

A starting point in developing that trust is to pray together. Pastors, encourage your elders to pray with you and for you, even if it feels awkward at first. A tradition at many congregations is for one of the elders to meet with the pastor(s) every Sunday morning before the Divine Service to share a devotion and prayer. They may even sing a hymn together. Elders, you do a tremendous service to pastors by praying with them and for them!

CARE FOR THE SPIRITUAL LIFE OF THE MEMBERS OF THE CONGREGATION

Elders are authorized to:

- "Care for their own spiritual life first of all (and of that of their families), being fully devoted to the means of grace. Be regular in church and communion attendance and faithful in Bible class attendance.

Practice faithfully the various aspects of stewardship: willing to use time, talents, and treasure in God's service."[3]

☐ Encourage all members to faithfully attend Divine Services and weekly Bible class.

☐ Be faithful in daily prayer for members of the congregation and others.

☐ Have a heart for those who are hurting within the congregation by providing genuine care for their spiritual well-being by making them aware of the seriousness of their sins and directing them to the Gospel for the forgiveness of sins.

Elders need to care for the spiritual welfare of others by being faithful in worship, Bible study, their service to others, and by being genuinely concerned about sin. Central to the Divine Service and spiritual care is the proclamation of the Gospel for the forgiveness of sins. This is the heart of spiritual care. John writes, "If we say we have no sin, we deceive ourselves, and the truth is not in us. If we confess our sins, He is faithful and just to forgive us our sins and to cleanse us from all unrighteousness. If we say we have not sinned, we make Him a liar, and His word is not in us" (1 John 1:8–10). James highlights the importance of confronting someone sinning when he says, "My brothers, if anyone among you wanders from the truth and someone brings him back, let him know that whoever brings back a sinner from his wandering will save his soul from death and will cover a multitude of sins" (James 5:19–20).

In general, people tend to minimize the seriousness of sin and its effect on their own lives and on the lives of others. Hence, there is no urgency about receiving the Gospel for the forgiveness of their sins in the Divine Service or privately before the pastor. There is also a reluctance to confront those who are sinning out of fear of being accused of being self-righteous. Yet, listen to what Jesus says about this: "If your brother sins against you, go and tell him his fault, between you and him alone. If he listens to you, you have gained your brother. But if he does not listen, take one or two others along with you, that every charge may be established by the evidence of two or three witnesses. If he refuses to listen to them, tell it to the church" (Matthew 18:15–17a). Johann Gerhard speaks about how we seem to be more concerned about a person's physical well-being than his or her spiritual well-being. In the following prayer of confession, Gerhard laments on how he participates in the sins of others by his failure to confront them in their sins:

> My neighbor dies a physical death, and I mourn and groan day and night, though physical death brings no harm to the godly person because it provides a transition to the heavenly kingdom. My neighbor dies a spiritual death by committing mortal sins, and I watch my neighbor die without concern. I am not grieved at all, though sin is the true death of the soul through which comes the inestimable loss of divine grace and eternal life. My neighbor offends the king, and I seek my neighbor's reconciliation by every means available. My neighbor offends the King of kings, who is able to dispatch soul and body to hell (Matthew 10:28), and I look on without concern. I do not consider this offense of the King to be an immeasurable evil. My neighbor stumbles on a stone, and I quickly prevent the fall or help my neighbor up from the fall. My neighbor stumbles on the Cornerstone of our salvation (Psalm 118:22), and I show careless neglect. Void of concern and attentiveness I ought to have, I do not lift up my neighbor again. My sins are many and weighty enough, but still I am not afraid to participate in someone else's sins.[4]

It is often even worse than that. Not only do we not say anything regarding the sins of our brothers and sisters in Christ, we bless them in their sinning by excusing it or justifying it. Elders need to speak the truth in love to those entrusted to their care so that those sinning repent of their sins and receive the Lord's forgiveness. "Brothers, if anyone is caught in any transgression, you who are spiritual should restore him in a spirit of gentleness" (Galatians 6:1). Elders, this is not just the work of the pastor; this is your work as a member of the priesthood of all believers and the board of elders.

A pastor always asks those in his new member classes, "How many Commandments do you think that I, the pastor, have broken?" Typically, they will answer two or three. It gets really fun when he asks them "which ones?" The correct answer is all of them. Jesus said, "You therefore must be perfect, as your heavenly Father is perfect" (Matthew 5:48). The truth is that we all fall short of following every commandment, whether in thought, word, or deed. Jesus summed up the Commandments by saying, "You shall love the Lord your God with all your heart and with all your soul and with all your mind. This is the great and first commandment. And a second is like it: You shall love your neighbor as yourself" (Matthew 22:37–39). We admit that we have broken every commandment when we confess in the Divine Service, "We have not loved You with our whole heart; we have not loved our neighbors as ourselves."[5] James also reminds us, "Whoever keeps the whole law but fails in one point has become accountable for all of it" (James 2:10). The only one who has followed every Commandment perfectly is Jesus Christ. This righteousness of Jesus Christ is given to us through the Gospel. Elders care for the spiritual life of the members of the congregation by pointing them to the Gospel of Jesus Christ for the forgiveness of sins.

INVOLVING MEMBERS OF THE CONGREGATION IN CHRISTIAN SERVICE

Service is important in the church! James writes, "But be doers of the word, and not hearers only, deceiving yourselves. For if anyone is a hearer of the word and not a doer, he is like a man who looks intently at his natural face in a mirror. For he looks at himself and goes away and at once forgets what he was like. But the one who looks into the perfect law, the law of liberty, and perseveres, being no hearer who forgets but a doer who acts, he will be blessed in his doing" (James 1:22–25).

Elders are authorized to:

- "Emphasize every-member participation in the work of the church. People have to be challenged, taught and led by being confronted with opportunities to get involved."[6]

- Encourage members to get involved in service by showing them how their talents and abilities could be used in service to the Lord and His Church.

We live in a world of busy people. Many parents and children don't even sit down to eat a meal together because Dad is working late, one of the children is at soccer, another is at volleyball, another is at a rehearsal for a play, and Mom is working at one of the concession stands at the school. Demands on one's time come from many different places, including the church. Unfortunately, the above scenario is what life for many looks like virtually every day of the week. This makes it difficult to find people interested in sitting on a board or committee of the congregation, especially if it competes with watching their children at sporting events, seeing them perform in the school play, or getting their children to and from various activities. Some congregations have cut back on the number of boards and committees and instead have focused on specific areas of service within the congregation. While they still have a board of elders and board of Christian day school, all other areas of ministry are directed from the church council, with one person on the council given a specific area of responsibility, such as evangelism, human care, youth, properties, stewardship, and Christian education. This means that instead of people having to commit to serving on a board or committee in one of these areas for two years, they may be called upon to help out with just one activity or more if it fits in with their schedule. This has lead to a greater variety of people getting involved because they are not locked into an area of service requiring a long-term commitment.

While it is important to make service opportunities known in the bulletins and newsletters of the congregation, it has greater impact if people are personally asked to serve. This is where elders can be of great assistance to the pastor. It is especially helpful because elders will probably be more aware of the talents, abilities, and interests of those in the congregation than other members of the congregation. A word of personal encouragement from an elder who is a fellow member of the congregation can in some cases be a more effective way of inviting others' participation than if that same invitation came from the pastor. Elders serve as role models for their service to others, and congregation members may be more apt to trust the commitment being asked for from an elder serving alongside them rather than being "talked into it" by a pastor desperate to fill the position by minimizing the time commitment involved.

WRITING, CALLING, AND VISITING MEMBERS

Elders are authorized to:

- Encourage families assigned to them to be faithful, send greetings to them about significant events in their lives, or share information concerning the church via e-mail, social networking, a note or card, a phone call, or a visit.

- Make visits, whenever possible, to new members, inactives, the sick, and shut-ins.

- Introduce new members to current members.

- Assist with assimilation of new members into the life of the church.

This is an area where many elders have difficulty. When writing, calling on, or visiting a member, especially one who has been inactive, what does an elder say and how will it be received? When writing, it is important to establish a tone of genuine care. Many see an elder contact as meaning that they have done something wrong or that they're being singled out. However, there may be something someone in the congregation has done that has led this person to be estranged from worship. In writing a letter to someone who has been inactive, elders need to keep that possibility in mind.

At my present church, we send a letter from the elders at the beginning of Advent and Lent every year. Included in this letter is a brochure with a general invitation to attend upcoming services, a few words about the season, and a list of the texts and themes of upcoming sermons. See Appendix B for examples of letters.

In the follow-up call or a cold call to a member, elders should begin by identifying themselves and greeting the person they are calling. Elders should proceed by stating the reason for the call and asking if it would be a convenient time to talk. If not, elders should ask if and when they might call at a later date. If the call proceeds, elders should remember that the main purpose of the call is to genuinely listen to the person. When appropriate, they should ask follow-up questions to understand more of what is going on in the person's life and how the elders might better serve his or her spiritual needs. Don't jump to conclusions, evaluate what the person is saying, or argue. Listen to learn and understand what is going on in the person's life.

When visiting, follow the same principle. Listen to others without evaluating what they are saying. Let them know that you are hearing what they are saying. Ask follow-up questions to get at the heart of what is going on. You don't need to try to solve the presenting problem, if there is one. Be yourself and genuine in your care and concern for the people's spiritual welfare. The most important thing you can do in a visit is to establish a trust and understanding with the people with whom you are visiting. Before leaving, you should ask if it would be all right to share with them a devotion and prayer.

In order for elders to feel comfortable writing, calling, or visiting members of the congregation, they are encouraged to practice and role-play various situations. The DVD vignettes for this book are intended to help in this area. Another helpful method to learn is for an elder to go with the pastor on visits. The pastor can model for the elder how visits are conducted, and with time and elder experience, the pastor can give more opportunities for the elder to assist him in the visit.

One of the easiest things an elder can do, and what has great impact, is simply to recognize what is going on in the lives of the people entrusted to his care. A short note that he is praying for the person or family and recognizing a birthday, anniversary, or a significant event in the person's life expresses care for that person. At our church, we have note cards with a picture of the church on the cover. Both elders and pastors are encouraged to use these cards to send brief notes to members of the church.

Often new members are not adequately assimilated into the life of the congregation. Elders need to be especially aware of how those who have been members for years may unknowingly discourage new members from getting involved and feeling at home in the congregation. In elder meetings, elders and pastors should talk about how to involve new members in activities and make an intentional effort to help them to feel at home.

In addition, there are times when active members become less active, especially if there are changes in their lives. For example, a member indicated that he and his wife were feeling less connected with the congregation over the period of a couple of years. In talking with them, they were able to pin-point that after their last child graduated from our school, they were no longer involved in anything in the congregation outside of the weekly Divine Service. They went from weekly activities with fellow members of the congregation through the school to not meeting socially with other members at all. Elders need to help families stay connected to the church when transitions take place, such as a marriage, change in employment, retirement, or death in the family, just to name a few.

Membership

Elders are authorized to

- meet regularly in order to properly care for the spiritual lives of members of the congregation;

- make appropriate recommendations to the church council regarding the reception of new members, peaceful releases, and the transfer of members;

- make sure that official records of the congregation are kept up-to-date and are stored safely.

Both pastor(s) and elders have a responsibility to meet regularly and to make board of elders meetings beneficial and effective so that the goal of caring for the church and one another is accomplished. This starts with the chairman preparing a written agenda for each meeting and following it. (For a sample of an elder agenda, see Appendix C.)

In order for an elder meeting to be effective, the chairman needs to make clear the purpose for the meeting through the agenda. Prepare the agenda well in advance of the meeting, get it to the elders and pastor(s) ahead of time, and make sure to follow it. In addition, consult the pastor(s) beforehand for any additions to the agenda. Recognize at the outset that it is very easy for someone to lead a meeting away from its stated purpose. The chairman needs to prevent this from happening so that the goals of the meeting are accomplished. This doesn't mean that other matters are not brought up, but that they are included in an orderly matter that fits with the agenda. Some tips on running an effective meeting:

- Make it timely. Always start the meeting on time even if some are late in arriving. Set a time limit on the meeting.

- Stay on topic. If, during the meeting, someone begins talking about things not pertinent to the issue being discussed, politely but firmly remind him of the agenda item under discussion. For example, you might say, "That's a good point you are making, but right now we are discussing the first item on the agenda."

- Let people have their say. There may be an elder or pastor who likes to argue about everything. Perhaps he just likes to play devil's advocate. Let him have his say, but then ask the other elders' opinion if it is pertinent to the subject at hand. Someone will usually respond in a way that gets the meeting back on track.

- Solicit input. One of the elders may not like to say anything but obviously has much to contribute or he wouldn't be on the board. It may be that he is shy or intimidated by speaking in front of others. A good way to get him involved in the conversation is to affirm him and ask if he'd like to share his opinion on a given issue. Or you might go around the table and ask each elder what he thinks about a particular issue.

In addition to the chairman providing a written agenda for the meeting, it is important for the pastor to provide a written report to the board of elders. A written report is preferable to an oral report. (For a sample of a pastor report, see Appendix D.)

The pastor report does not reveal sensitive, confidential information, nor does it need to list every mundane detail of what the pastor does each day. The report is not for the purpose of justifying what the pastor does. It does, however, assist the pastor and elders in assessing how the pastor is using his time relative to what he has been called and ordained to do within the congregation. It is very easy to get sidetracked from Word and Sacrament ministry to spending all one's time on administrative and organizational tasks. This issue is nothing new. Hermann Sasse warned about this many years ago when he identified how the influence of a business model in the church can divert the pastor from his calling as a pastor:

> To proclaim the Gospel of forgiveness, to declare to repentant sinners the forgiveness of their sins, to distribute the Sacraments with all the gifts of divine grace contained in them, this and nothing else, is the proper task of the minister of Christ as it was the *officium proprium* ["proper office"] of Christ himself. . . . The church administration in Europe follows the patterns of the administration of the state, while in America the great business organizations seem to be unknowingly imitated by the churches. The consequence is that also the parish minister becomes more and more of an administrator and organizer who rushes from meeting to meeting and has not enough time for his proper calling as a shepherd."[7]

A written pastor report can assist the elders in helping the pastor to stay focused on what he has been called and ordained to do within the congregation: namely, Word and Sacrament ministry.

Both pastor(s) and elders need to keep accurate records about members of the congregation. Church records are important, but even something as simple as keeping updated records of member addresses can be challenging because most people these days do not take the time or recognize the need of informing the church even about an address change. A change of a phone number or e-mail address is even more difficult to keep up with, especially in larger congregations, as cell phone numbers, for example, are not publicly listed. Often congregations find out about a change of address via the newsletter being returned in the mail.

It is also important to talk about transfers or releases in an elder meeting. Sometimes even pastors recommend transfers or releases without much thought about the spiritual welfare of those being transferred or released. It is not uncommon, especially in larger congregations, to simply receive a letter of transfer from another congregation concerning a family who are members of your congregation. Approval of the transfer is often done with without any questions being asked. In some cases, there may be a spiritual issue involved and the person or family is simply running away from it. Congregations should not be enabling such sinful behavior. Before transferring or releasing a member, the matter needs to be resolved and reconciled through the forgiveness of Christ.

Elders need to ask why a person or family is transferring. There are times when it should not be approved. But when a transfer or release occurs for less than pious reasons, it is important for elders and pastors not to demonize those leaving. It may be personally hurtful to you when someone leaves a congregation for reasons that seem petty or unloving, but there is often other things going on in the life of that person or family. Instead of being angry, leave the door open for them to return. Be gracious and understanding, especially because they may need your help later on. James offers some helpful advice here, "Know this, my beloved brothers: let every person be quick to hear, slow to speak, slow to anger; for the anger of man does not produce the righteousness of God" (James 1:19–20).

FOR REFLECTION AND DISCUSSION

1. Why is the worship and devotional life of elders of utmost importance?

2. What are the qualifications of an elder?

3. List things elders should be doing at every Divine Service to assist the pastor.

4. How can the board of elders show genuine care for the pastor?

5. Why is it caring to confront someone who is sinning, and how can a pastor or elder do it without appearing self-righteous?

6. What are characteristics of an effective letter, call, or visit made by an elder to a member of the congregation?

7. How can the elders help assimilate new members into the congregation and assist in keeping families connected to the church?

8. Why are written agendas and pastor reports important for elder meetings?

9. How can pastors and elders make elder meetings more effective and involve everyone in the meeting?

10. How should transfers and releases be handled in elder meetings?

BUILDING TRUST BETWEEN PASTORS AND ELDERS

Chapter THREE

So if there is any encouragement in Christ, any comfort from love, any participation in the Spirit, any affection and sympathy, complete my joy by being of the same mind, having the same love, being in full accord and of one mind. Do nothing from rivalry or conceit, but in humility count others more significant than yourselves.

—Philippians 2:1–3

In the passage above, St. Paul urges God's people in Christ to work together. In order for us as fellow believers in Christ to do this, it is important for us to trust one another. Unfortunately, there is much mistrust, not only in the world but also among those in the Church. A lack of trust has caused many storms of anger and conflict, especially between many pastors and elders. Our anger churns when a confidence is broken or when a pastor or elder does something wrong or hurtful to us, especially when it is done behind our backs. In the midst of this wind of rage and these waves of dissension, we need to recognize the presence of Christ among us through the Gospel to reconcile us through the forgiveness of sins. Jesus said, "Peace I leave with you; My peace I give to you. Not as the world gives do I give to you. Let not your hearts be troubled, neither let them be afraid" (John 14:27).

Instead of running away from conflict or demonizing the pastor or elder with whom we disagree, we, as Christians, are encouraged to speak to one another without sacrificing either the truth or love. The apostle Paul writes that we are no longer to be like children "tossed to and fro by the waves and carried about by every wind of doctrine, by human cunning, by craftiness in deceitful schemes. Rather, speaking the truth in love, we are to grow up in every way into Him who is the head, into Christ, from whom the whole body, joined and held together by every joint with which it is equipped, when each part is working properly, makes the body grow so that it builds itself up in love" (Ephesians 4:14–16).

In Matthew 14, we learn how Jesus was involved not only in the lives of the disciples but also how He is involved in our lives today. In that chapter, we hear how Jesus made the disciples get into a boat while He ascended a mountain to pray. Think of the boat as the Church. The place where you sit in church on Sunday is called the nave, a Latin term which by no small coincidence means "boat." Now that Jesus has ascended into heaven, He is doing for us what He did for those disciples who were in the boat in the midst of the wind and waves of a storm. He is interceding on our behalf before our Father in heaven. He is praying that His Word would have its way in our lives.

While looking out for the disciples, He knew they needed His help, and He went out to them in a miraculous way by walking on the water. Thinking He was a ghost, the disciples were terrified, but Jesus said,

> "Take heart; it is I. Do not be afraid." And Peter answered Him, "Lord, if it is You, command me to come to You on the water." He said, "Come." So Peter got out of the boat and walked on the water and came to Jesus. But when he saw the wind, he was afraid, and beginning to sink he cried out, "Lord, save me." Jesus immediately reached out His hand and took hold of him, saying to him, "O you of little faith, why did you doubt?" And when they got into the boat, the wind ceased. And those in the boat worshiped Him, saying, "Truly You are the Son of God." (Matthew 14:27–33)

When Peter fixed his eyes on Jesus, the author and perfecter of our faith, he did what was thought to be impossible. Peter walked on water. But when the wind diverted his view of Jesus, he began to sink into the troubled waters of doubt and despair. But Jesus would not allow Peter to sink into those waters. Jesus "reached out His hand and took hold of him."

Think for a moment of what Jesus has promised you. "My sheep hear My voice, and I know them, and they follow Me. I give them eternal life, and they will never perish, and no one will snatch them out of My hand" (John 10:27–28). Peter's feeble trust did not prevent Jesus from saving him. Jesus took hold of him, put him into the boat, and the storm ceased. There was peace—as there always is when Jesus intervenes.

When they had been saved, those in the boat worshiped Jesus. It is also what we do today in the boat of the Lord's Church. His ascension does not mean absence; Jesus still comes to us in a miraculous way on the water. He's the word in the water of our Baptism, and He brings peace to our stormy conflicts through the forgiveness of sins. Pastors and elders are put back into the boat of the Church not only strengthened in their faith and trust in Jesus, but through His peace are also strengthened in their trust in one another as members of the Body of Christ.

In order for trust to develop between elders and pastors, not only do they need to hear the Word of God together, receiving that encouragement of Christ, but they also need to get to know one another. Elders and pastors need to take time to talk with one another and learn about what is going on in one another's lives and with their families. A great way to do that is to get together socially. Plan a trip to a ball game, a dinner together, or other activities that assist you in building relationships outside of your responsibilities as an elder or pastor. On occasion after elder meetings, go out for a "Lutheran beverage" or soda together. It is a great way to build a healthy working relationship. This assists in recognizing that each person on the board of elders along with the pastor(s) is significant, someone whom God has put in your path to serve and care for and to work alongside in the kingdom of God.

We saw above St. Paul's words about the importance of "being in full accord and of one mind." This happens as the Word of God gives you the mind of Christ so that you work together, care for one another, and recognize that each of you brings something different and unique in service to the Lord and His Church.

Sometimes difficulties in relationships between elders and pastors occur not due to a specific sin, but because of a clash of differing personality styles. Understanding the influence of our different personality styles can be helpful in developing trust between pastors and elders. It can assist us in understanding how others perceive things and how best to relate to them. There are many research studies that have analyzed relational patterns and a variety of ways of categorizing personality styles, but generally speaking, we all possess four different personality styles. There is no best or worst style, since all personality styles are effective when appropriate to the situation and are implemented well.

It needs to be understood that categorizing personality styles is a guide to assist in relating to and understanding another person, and not a means of stereotyping that person. There are combinations of styles, and a particular style might be more dominant in one area of life, such as at work, while another style may be more dominant at home. While many people have categorized the four personality styles in a variety of ways, I have categorized them as follows: doer, charmer, connector, and perfectionist.

The Doer: Action Oriented

A doer, as the name implies, gets things done. He or she is highly effective in accomplishing tasks and in reaching goals. A doer will push others to get things done quickly and efficiently by whatever means possible. A doer is typically not concerned about people, only results. A doer is not usually a good listener because he already knows what he's going to do; he wants things done his way. A doer may be involved in several different tasks at once, performing well in all of them. However, if a doer takes on too many responsibilities, he or she can be overwhelmed and may walk away from them all. A doer is highly competitive and wants to win no matter what the cost.

The strength of this personality style is the ability to get things done in an effective manner. People with a doer personality style tend to make great administrators. An elder with this style, for example, is not going to let a meeting go on and on without accomplishing specific goals. A pastor with this style may find it easier to communicate the Gospel in a clear and effective way. Doers are decisive and typically natural leaders.

Understanding this personality style can help address certain issues when things go wrong. A member of the congregation complained to an elder, "I quit going to church because Pastor doesn't care about me. Several months ago we ran into each other and he walked right by me without even saying hello." Of course, it is unfortunate for something like this to take place, but it is not uncharacteristic of a pastor who has a doer personality. It is entirely possible that in his haste to get things done, he never saw the person or, if he did, didn't see exchanging pleasantries as important as accomplishing the work he had scheduled for the day. The same thing could happen within a meeting with elders. The pastor or an elder with this personality style may become impatient with others in meetings, and, as a result, may end up being offensive to some.

To communicate successfully with a pastor or elder with this personality style, be short and to the point, because their strong orientation toward decisive action tends to make doers impatient. When communicating with a doer, help him connect being personable with achieving results. For example, in relationships with others, it can be pointed out to a pastor with a doer personality style that he will be more effective in proclaiming the Gospel to others by taking the time to talk with people. Make him aware of how a failure to acknowledge people around him makes him less effective. In addition, be aware that doers may also take on too many challenges and responsibilities, and if the pressure becomes too great, they may drop everything and walk away. Doers are task and goal oriented and want to see results. Obstacles that stand in the way of goal achievement can be both discouraging and frustrating for them.

The Charmer: Intuition Oriented

A charmer is a people person. He loves people and likes to visit with them. People are drawn to such a person and feel comfortable with him almost instantly. A charmer loves to talk and will be very engaging with the people around him. A charmer naturally shares his feelings about things with others and in doing so creates a bond with them—though that bond may end up being short-lived.

The strength of the charmer personality style for a pastor or elder is that, unlike the doer style, he can be very approachable. People will feel close to him, and feel that they can trust and confide in him. Pastors and elders whose dominant personality style is that of a charmer typically love people and can be fun to be around. They are often creative, outgoing optimists who may be the life of the party and whose presence in a room is recognized immediately.

A weakness of this style is follow-through on accomplishing tasks in a timely manner. Where the doer utilizes decisive actions to accomplish his goals, the charmer intuitively fosters relationships to do the same, but those goals are accomplished at a much slower rate, and sometimes fail to get done. This is why those with this particular style of personality tend to be "social butterflies." Charmers may even end up having to reschedule appointments because they spend so much time visiting that they lose track of time.

THE CONNECTOR: RELATIONSHIP ORIENTED

A connecter wants everyone to work well together. A connector is a team player and works to keep everyone happy. He will genuinely seek to understand people and what they are going through so that they feel a part of the team. A connector is often a middle child. His office will typically be filled with a lot pictures of his family. He also seeks acceptance and approval of others.

A pastor or elder with an connector personality style typically wants everyone to get along. A strength of a pastor or elder with this style is that he is typically a good listener, loyal, likeable, and trustworthy. He can be effective at getting people to work together for the good of all. A potential weakness, however, is that he will tend to avoid conflict, preferring to just smooth things over with those who are at odds. The pastor or elder with this style of personality may be reluctant, for example, to confront those who need to repent of their sin. Finally, because of their strong emphasis on cooperative friendships, connectors may also be very sensitive to criticism. In working with connectors it is important to give encouragement to them and to recognize their accomplishments.

THE PERFECTIONIST: THINKING ORIENTED

A perfectionist, as the name implies, is concerned about everything being correct. Unlike the doer, who wants to get things done, a perfectionist is more concerned with getting things right. Perfectionists tend to focus on details.

A perfectionist may seem hard to get to know at first because his focus is on facts, not people. In working with a perfectionist, take time to get to know him or her, because, unlike the charmer, he or she may not be someone who seems very warm or engaging, especially at first.

The strength of this personality style is attention to details and making sure that what is decided will be beneficial to the congregation. The perfectionist pastor or elder will be more likely to make sure that sound data supports the decisions that are made. He will help ward off mistakes made by overly optimistic assumptions. A pastor or elder with a perfectionist personality style is often an excellent problem-solver and an asset to the work of the board. Yet an elder or pastor with this personality style may frustrate an elder or pastor with a doer personality because the perfectionist can be very slow to act. His attention to order and accuracy may cause meetings to go long, and his attention to detail may give the impression that he prefers data to people.

In this brief overview of personality styles, it is easy to see how a clash of personality styles can breed mistrust among pastors, elders, and other members of the congregation. Understanding our differing personality styles, along with the strengths and weaknesses associated with them, can assist in building much needed trust between pastors and elders.

EMOTIONAL INTELLIGENCE

Improving one's emotional intelligence (also known as EQ or Emotional Quotient) can assist in building relationships and trust between pastors and elders. Emotional intelligence is one's personal competence in the areas of self-awareness and self-management, and social competence in the areas of social awareness and relationship management.

> Self-awareness is your ability to accurately perceive your emotions and stay aware of them as they happen. This includes keeping on top of how you tend to respond to specific situations and certain people.

> Self-management is your ability to use awareness of your emotions to stay flexible and positively direct your behavior. This

means managing your emotional reactions to all situations and people.

Social awareness is your ability to accurately pick up emotions in other people and get what is really going on. This often means understanding what other people are thinking and feeling even if you don't feel the same way.

Relationship management is your ability to use awareness of your emotions and the emotions of others to manage interactions successfully. Letting emotional awareness guide clear communication and effective handling of conflict.[1]

We hear almost daily about people failing to control their emotions by losing their temper or becoming enraged over even the most mundane things. For example, there are so many people who fail to control their emotions while driving that the phrase "road rage" has become common to our vocabulary. Such loss of emotional control is not only happening on the road, however, it is also happening in the Church. Church rage is doing great damage to our trust of one another as members of the Body of Christ. It is a fruit of our fallen nature that is rotten to the core.

When you get upset about something or are surprised by something that has happened, are you aware of how this affects you emotionally? If you are, you can manage it better and do a better job of refraining from saying something you might later regret, especially if you are angry. A way to self-manage your behavior in an emotionally charged situation might be to take a deep breath or count to ten before saying anything. It is also important to pick up on the emotions of others. Their tone of voice, body language, and way of speaking can give you clues about whether or not the matter you are dealing with is one that is personally upsetting to the person. Being aware of the emotions involved in a given situation can assist you in resolving a particular conflict instead of making it worse to the point of damaging your trust in each other.

The simple fact is that our emotions change when we are upset. We can either be controlled by them or learn to control them. The good news concerning emotional intelligence is you can become more emotionally aware in your relationships with others and thus enhance your trust of one another. Even more important to gaining that emotional control is your participation in the things of the Spirit of God, namely, the Lord's Word and Sacrament. The apostle Paul writes,

> Now the works of the flesh are evident: sexual immorality, impurity, sensuality, idolatry, sorcery, enmity, strife, jealousy, fits of anger, rivalries, dissensions, divisions, envy, drunkenness, orgies, and things like these. I warn you, as I warned you before, that those who do such things will not inherit the kingdom of God. But the fruit of the Spirit is love, joy, peace, patience, kindness, goodness, faithfulness, gentleness, self-control; against such things there is no law. And those who belong to Christ Jesus have crucified the flesh with its passions and desires.
>
> If we live by the Spirit, let us also walk by the Spirit. Let us not become conceited, provoking one another, envying one another. (Galatians 5:19–26)

In addition to understanding different personality styles and becoming more emotionally intelligent, there are many outside organizations that can assist in building trust between pastors and elders and make them more effective in working together for the sake of the church. Talk to your circuit counselor or district president about programs available within your circuit or district. One such program is called Doxology: The Lutheran Center for Spiritual Care and Counsel, which is a recognized service organization of The Lutheran Church—Missouri Synod.

> DOXOLOGY offers an innovative program of advanced study retreats to strengthen pastors for the task of faithfully shepherding the souls entrusted to their care. DOXOLOGY provides pastors with a unique study and renewal experience, rooted in the classic art of spiritual care and informed by the insights of contemporary Christian psychology. (www.doxology.us)

Unfortunately, there are many pastors who think their elders and congregation members wouldn't be interested in such care for them as pastors. Whether true or not, it does signal that many pastors and elders are not "in full accord and of one mind." Building trust in ways such as this is needed, especially given the individualist culture in which we live.

For pastors there are times when the challenges and difficulties of ministry seem overwhelming. It is very easy for them to get burned out by trying to meet everyone's expectations. It is important for pastors to trust their elders with their frustrations, concerns, failures, and even their sins. Many pastors tend to see their elders more as those to whom they need to justify their actions. Instead, elders should be recognized for who they are, namely, brothers in Christ. If pastors genuinely entrust to their elders what is going on with them, they will be blessed. Elders are there to build pastors up with the Gospel, as the pastors have done for them. Pastors, elders will forgive you, encourage you, and remind you that you are not, for example, called to meet everyone's expectations. You are called to preach, teach, and care for others by faithfully proclaiming the Gospel of Jesus Christ in word and deed. By opening up with elders they will become more open with you.

In Psalm 139:1–3, David speaks of how frightening it is to trust another with such an in-depth knowledge of you:

> O LORD, You have searched me and known me. You know when I
> sit down and when I rise up; You discern my thoughts from afar.
> You search out my path and my lying down and are acquainted
> with all my ways.

God sees everything—every thought, every word, everything we have ever done. It is really scary to think about, especially when we ponder all of our sinful thoughts, words, and deeds. We have a natural desire to hide those things because we think that if they become known, we will not be accepted, loved, and cared for by God or others. But the Gospel is this: God knew all about our sins beforehand, and this is precisely why He sent His Son, Jesus Christ, into the world. This is good news because we learn that, in Christ, God doesn't stop loving us because of what we do. He doesn't love us because of what we don't do. He loves us because of who we are: His dear children. With that encouragement of Christ and that comfort from His love, we are enabled to love one another as He has first loved us—not for what we do or don't do, but for who we are: children of God.

FOR REFLECTION AND DISCUSSION

1. Why is it important for pastors and elder to trust in one another?

2. What are some of the reasons for a breakdown in trust between pastors and elders?

3. What are the characteristics of the four main personality styles?

4. What is Emotional Intelligence (EQ) and how can it be helpful in maintaining trust between elders and pastors?

5. Take a personality style inventory. What is your dominant personality style?

6. Fill out a peer personality style inventory on a fellow elder or the pastor. What is his dominant personality style from your perspective?

7. Compare your personal style inventory with the one filled out about you by one of your peers on the board of elders, and with everyone on the board of elders, including the pastor(s).

8. Review personality style descriptions.

9. Discuss the five most pressing needs of pastors (see Appendix F).

Chapter FOUR

Do not be conformed to this world, but be transformed by the renewal of your mind, that by testing you may discern what is the will of God, what is good and acceptable and perfect.

—Romans 12:2

Following a high school track meet, the team was waiting for the coach to return. The conversation among members of the team turned to what some of the guys were going to do that night. One guy said he was going out on the town for a night of "wine, women, and song." When someone said in surprise that he thought this track member was Roman Catholic, the guy replied that was not a problem since he would go to confession the next day and be forgiven. A Lutheran on the bus boasted that even though he was going out to do the same thing, he didn't need to bother with confession because he was "saved by grace through faith." And yet neither properly understood faith or forgiveness. Both the Lutheran and the Roman Catholic had perverted the Gospel. They were conformed to the world in such a way that they thought they could use even the Gospel to serve their own ends.

Many in today's culture have an entitlement mentality even when it comes to the things of God and His Church. There is a belief among some that the pastor is only there to hatch (baptize), match (marry), and dispatch (bury) members of the church. They want it their way, not God's way. This presents a huge challenge for both pastors and elders in caring for the church. Even within the church, many see the pastor as someone who is just there to give them what they want, nothing more and nothing less. It is part of the consumerist culture in which we live.

Consider Baptism, for example. Many want their child baptized but have no intention of bringing the child to the weekly services of God's house. However, the faith created in the child by the water and word of Holy Baptism needs to be fed, nourished, and sustained by the Gospel. It is why parents are asked to promise to be faithful in bringing their child(ren) to the weekly Divine Service. It is also why sponsors are chosen. They are, by their words and deeds, to encourage the child being baptized to be faithful in receiving the Lord's Word and Sacrament. In the service of Holy Baptism there is a clear statement of what sponsors are to do:

> From ancient times the Church has observed the custom of ap-
> pointing sponsors for baptismal candidates and catechumens.
> In the Evangelical Lutheran Church sponsors are to confess the
> faith expressed in the Apostles' Creed and taught in the Small
> Catechism. They are, whenever possible, to witness the Baptism
> of those they sponsor. They are to pray for them, support them in
> their ongoing instruction and nurture in the Christian faith, and
> encourage them toward the faithful reception of the Lord's Sup-
> per. They are at all times to be examples to them of the holy life of
> faith in Christ and love for the neighbor. (*LSB*, p. 269)

Unfortunately, many sponsors are chosen not for their faithfulness to the Lord's Word but because they are friends or members of the same family. Many who are not as active in the church politely listen to the teaching about Baptism and the importance of feeding the faith created in Baptism only to disappear until Christmas, Easter, or when someone in the family would like to be married or needs to be buried. Instead of being transformed by the love of God in Jesus Christ, they reject the Gospel by remaining conformed to the way of a fallen, consumerist world.

There is a real disconnect today among Christians between what is said and done, even among those who have attended Lutheran schools from preschool through college. Many fail to take the Gospel seriously and have returned to conformity with the unholy trinity of the devil, world, and their own sinful selves. Take marriage, for example. At one particular wedding reception, a pastor found out from an intoxicated maid of honor's toast that the bride and groom had been living together for five years. It was clear from the look of guilt on the faces of the bride's parents that not only had they known about it, but that they were in on the lie and had covered it up to the pastor. The grandmother sitting next to the pastor asked him what he thought about couples living together before marriage; she didn't see it as a problem. Life in this self-absorbed fallen world has created a culture where there is fear of embarrassment, but no fear of God.

Instead of looking to the Lord who instituted holy marriage to define what it is, a self-absorbed culture redefines marriage as a mere personal contract between a man and woman to be honored as long as they both shall will. Some are even questioning the need for marriage: a recent news report on NBC revealed that 40 percent of those surveyed think marriage is obsolete. The culture has lost the truth that a husband and wife are icons of Christ the bridegroom, and the Church, His bride.

Divorce is prevalent even among us Christians even though God hates divorce. Likewise, most couples that have been divorced hate it too. One of the devastating effects of divorce is that it may cause you to question whether or not someone will ever genuinely love you, or even whether there is such a thing as true love. Worse, since marriage is an icon of your relationship with Christ, divorce may even cause you to question God's love for you in Jesus Christ. Is this the promise of happiness that a culture of consumerism has promised? Hardly. Thank God Jesus will never divorce you. His love abides through the forgiveness of sins even in the midst of tragedies such as divorce. Perhaps we should remember there are reasons Jesus said, "What therefore God has joined together, let not man separate" (Matthew 19:6).

Obviously, divorce is also difficult for children. One of the lessons children learn from divorce is that when troubles come, there is always the option to just leave. Instead of having the love of God in Christ passed on to them, a love that "bears all things, believes all things, hopes all things, endures all things" (1 Corinthians 13:7), they are often left to experience the emptiness caused by the culture's emphasis upon love of self.

Marriage and family, as God has instituted them, have at their root self-sacrifice, self-denial, and service willingly given to another. And yet they have so much more to offer than does the culture of self-love. In the marriage service found in *Lutheran Service Book*, we hear a summary of what God in His

Word has to say about marriage:

> In marriage we see a picture of the communion between Christ and His bride, the Church. Our Lord blessed and honored marriage with His presence and first miracle at Cana in Galilee. This estate is also commended to us by the apostle Paul as good and honorable. Therefore, marriage is not to be entered into inadvisedly or lightly, but reverently, deliberately, and in accordance with the purposes for which it was instituted by God.
>
> The union of husband and wife in heart, body, and mind is intended by God for the mutual companionship, help, and support that each person ought to receive from the other, both in prosperity and adversity. Marriage was also ordained so that man and woman may find delight in one another. Therefore, all persons who marry shall take a spouse in holiness and honor, not in the passion of lust, for God has not called us to impurity but in holiness. God also established marriage for the procreation of children who are to be brought up in the fear and instruction of the Lord so that they may offer Him their praise. (*LSB*, p. 275)

We want it our way when it comes to funerals too. Some have fallen so far under the spell of the self-absorbed culture that they fail to see beyond themselves to recognize the importance of God's Word, even when confronted with death. A woman asked the pastor to conduct the funeral of her husband. In the ensuing discussion, it became clear to the pastor that her husband was still alive and was in the hospital. He asked if he could visit with the man to give him the comfort of God's Word. But that was not what she wanted. She just wanted the pastor to commit to conducting the funeral. Notice the failure to recognize her husband's need of the grace of God in Jesus Christ as he faced death.

The pastor refused to give in to the demands of the culture, and instead lived according to the Word of God and visited the dying man. When the pastor walked into the hospital room, the dying man said, "Go to hell and get the hell out of my room!" The pastor stayed, and for a while had a heated exchange with the man. He told the pastor that the church was full of hypocrites. The pastor told him that he should join us then because we could use another one. The pastor shared that the only one in the Church who wasn't a hypocrite, who said what He did and did what He said, was Jesus Christ, and that our salvation was found in Him alone. In the pastor's repeated visits with the man it became clear that his anger at God was misplaced, and in fact centered on what he had experienced in war many years before. The pastor was able to share with him the meaning of our Lord's suffering and death and finally, at long last, the man was released from his past as he received the Lord's Gospel gifts of forgiveness, life, and peace.

At his funeral, the pastor related this story about the first time he had met him. When he shared that the man had told him to go to hell, the room erupted with laughter because they all knew him well and what he had previously believed about God. The pastor was then able to share with them that the man eventually received the salvation won for him and for us all through the suffering, death and resurrection of Jesus Christ. The world's culture of self-absorption had left the man bitter and angry, but Christ's message of His self-sacrifice had given the man eternal peace. "For God so loved the world, that He gave His only Son, that whoever believes in Him should not perish but have eternal life. For God did not send His Son into the world to condemn the world, but in order that the world might be saved through Him" (John 3:16–17).

Another huge challenge for pastors and elders in their care of the church in this self-absorbed culture is athletics. Children in grade school and young men and women in high school are not only playing sports for their school teams but also club teams. In order to play against the best competition available, these teams will often travel across the country. Many, if not most, of these teams play on Sundays, including Sunday mornings. This has taken a large number of children and their families out of the Divine Service on a regular basis. Rick Reilly wrote an article for *Sports Illustrated* on April 26, 2004, entitled, "Let us ~~Pray~~ Play" addressing this very issue. You know it's bad when even a sportswriter recognizes that sports have taken over the Lord's Day.

"Remember the Sabbath day by keeping it holy. What does this mean? We should fear and love God so that we do not despise preaching and His

Word, but hold it sacred and gladly hear and learn it" (Small Catechism, Third Commandment). Given our society's preoccupation with sports it seems that the popular sports phrase "no fear" can be expanded to include "no fear of the Lord." The problem is that even parents are unknowingly teaching this to their children when they allow sports programs and its coaches to dictate their child(ren)'s schedule for the week. It is bad enough that children come back to school after a weekend of multiple games and hundreds of miles of travel exhausted and ill-prepared for their academic work at school. What is worse is that it is almost impossible for families to faithfully attend worship each week. This is the case even for members of congregations that offer Divine Services on different days of the week. The problem then is that God and His Word proclaimed to us in the Divine Service disrupts practice schedules.

A pastor sought to deal with his own daughter's volleyball club team's intrusion on Sunday morning worship by writing the following letter to the coach:

Dear [Coach],

I understand that you probably do not have much control over when our volleyball tournaments are played, but I would like to voice my displeasure with so many of the tournaments occurring on Sunday. Maybe you can at least let those in charge know that there is concern. I am hoping that they would consider starting tournaments later in the afternoon. I checked with those who played last year and they said that only two tournaments were played on Sunday. This year there are several more. The potential conflict with faithful church attendance is something we talked about with our daughter before allowing her to play on the club volleyball team. As a pastor, I am very concerned about how many of our young people are missing church throughout the year because of tournaments for volleyball, basketball, bowling, soccer, etc. I am not alone. This has become such a concern that many of us pastors are meeting to discuss how to address the issue. We certainly know that anyone is free to conduct tournaments anytime they please. We also, though, feel strongly enough about this to encourage parents not to participate if it is a choice between church and sports. As a longtime athlete and sports enthusiast I would rather work together so that there is mutual respect and support for both. Again, I don't know if you have any control over this, but please voice my concerns to those who do.

This particular coach responded to the letter above with the following:

Thank you for your input. I realize that Sundays can cause issues with some religious activities, and I apologize if this causes an issue. There are Saturday tournaments, but in the past we ran into many conflicts with basketball tournaments, since a good number of the girls play both sports. Once again, I am sorry for the conflict and will keep this in mind and discuss it with the coaches for next year.

Notice that the reason for playing on Sunday was that the girls were playing on more than one club team to the exclusion of other activities, most importantly, to the exclusion of faithfully receiving the Lord's gifts in the Divine Service.

The secular world has course disregard for not only Sundays but also other important days in the Church Year. When opening day of the major league baseball season took place on Good Friday, some of our members were at the local baseball game. When it was pointed out that they could still make it back for one of the Good Friday services, the response of some was that it was too much for one day.

Likewise, when the favorite NFL team played on Christmas Eve, there was a decline in attendance at the Divine Services that year, even though there were other opportunities for those attending the game to go to church later that night! The response of one family was that it was their family tradition to go to the 4 p.m. Divine Service and that's why they didn't attend the 6 p.m. or the 10 p.m. service that night, or the Christmas festival service the next day. The culture of self-absorption apparently taught them it was worth it to change their tradition for a game, but not for the Word of God. The issue here is not one of enjoying or valuing sports. The issue here is one of balance. It is important to acknowledge the imbalance of an exaggerated emphasis placed upon sports as the serious problem it is for our life together in Christ. There is no recognition of how one's absence adversely affects both a person's individual faith and our life together as the Body of Christ.

The "it's all about me" entitlement mentality is also being taught to our children by discouraging the importance of serving others. At one Lutheran school, two children each lunch period are asked to assist with preparing for the next group at lunch by wiping off the tables before heading out to recess. It is a simple task that teaches service. A new child to the school was asked to do this but refused, saying, "I don't clean tables." He asked to call his mother because, for him, this was a big issue. The mother, like her son, thought this to be a terrible thing to ask of a child. She came that very hour and pulled him out of the school. This child, his mother, and many within our culture of today have been taught to believe we are not to serve, but rather we are to be served by others.

These are very challenging times for the church. Rev. Dale A. Meyer, President of Concordia Seminary, St. Louis, Missouri, writes:

> "For some time now I've found The Lutheran Church—Missouri Synod a sad place. Many faithful pastors and people see church attendance declining. Many congregations are struggling to keep their doors open, but we regularly hear of church doors closing forever. Many rural congregations are dying, and few urban congregations are thriving. The strong witness of our Lutheran grade schools and high schools grows weaker by the year. Pre-seminary enrollments in the Concordia University System are drastically down, and declining residential enrollments at our seminaries are an ominous trend. Try as we do, and people are trying hard to get things going, we are up against cultural changes the likes of which we haven't seen in our lifetimes."[1]

President Meyer, despite the challenges, is hopeful for the future if we get back to trusting in the creative power and authority of the Word of God. He writes:

> We all try to peer into the future; that's human nature and can be good stewardship, but the best guidance for the uncertain future comes from the past. "This is what the Lord says, 'Stand at

the crossroads and look; ask for the ancient paths, ask where the good way is, and walk in it, and you will find rest for your souls' " (Jer 6:16). . . . I remember Martin Scharlemann saying, "God has given us the terrible ability to say, 'No.' to him." I am very positive about the future of The Lutheran Church—Missouri Synod if . . . if we humble ourselves and seek the whole counsel of God. . . . In the pastor's study, in the homes of all the baptized, in small group Bible studies, and in our life's centerpiece, the divine service, studying, hearing, and obeying the whole counsel of God should be our occupation."[2]

This is not just the work of the pastor, it is also the occupation of the elder. As elders, you are on the front lines to make it the occupation of all the members of the Body of Christ! When people say to you, for example, that they think the pastors shouldn't stress the importance of Bible study so much, you need not only to defend the teaching of God's Word but also talk to them about what a difference it makes in our lives. Invite them to attend with you. Many members of our congregations come in and go out of the Divine Service without ever even talking to others. Stop them, talk to them, and invite them to join you in the study of God's Word. When people say that they're not interested in a particular topic of Bible study, make them aware of the fact that it very well may be that when they go they will learn something interesting and new. By attending they will also assist others in growing in their knowledge and understanding of the Word of God. In Bible studies, assist the pastor in being aware of the questions and concerns of those attending the study. A frustration of many pastors is that so many people make judgments about Bible studies even though they haven't attended one in years, if ever. Elders, your pastors need your help here!

The answer to the challenge for the Church in this self-absorbed culture is found where it is has always been found, in the Word of God. Interesting, isn't it? That almost all of the problems we face in the church and in everyday life have to do with our being disconnected from the Word of God in one way or another? We need more of the Word of God in our lives, not less.

> Hear, O Israel: The LORD our God, the LORD is one. You shall love
> the LORD your God with all your heart and with all your soul and

with all your might. And these words that I command you today shall be on your heart. You shall teach them diligently to your children, and shall talk of them when you sit in your house, and when you walk by the way, and when you lie down, and when you rise. You shall bind them as a sign on your hand, and they shall be as frontlets between your eyes. You shall write them on the doorposts of your house and on your gates. (Deuteronomy 6:4–9)

As pastors and elders, we need to allow the Word of God to fill us with the Lord's gifts. In the passage above, notice how God's Word was primary in daily life. God's people and their children were taught to meditate on God's Word. Pastors and elders, likewise, should be meditating on the Word of God morning, noon, and night, and need to teach those entrusted to their care to do the same.

Everyone is engaged in meditation, whether conscious of it or not. The question has to do with what we are meditating on. Our daily meditation typically centers on ourselves—on what we are doing or on what others have done to us. In meditating on what others have done to us, we tend to focus in on how they have hurt us, and we replay that over and over in our minds. Christian meditation has its focus not on us, but on Christ and what He has done and continues to do for us, in us, and through us for others.

> Christian meditation differs from all other kinds of meditation because it concentrates on what Jesus says; it is meditation on His Word as it is given to us in the Scriptures [cf Dt. 6:6]. We meditate on His powerful Word. His Word has an impact on us as we pay attention to it, does its work in us as we listen to it, and reshapes us inwardly as we let it have its say. The words of Jesus actually produce our meditation. Yet that does not happen automatically but only as we put our trust in it.[3]

Begin early on with shaping and forming the people of God with the Word of God. The Green Sheet (Appendix A) keeps the Word of God in front of people daily. In our Lutheran schools, for example, throughout the year many follow a "learn-by-heart schedule" like the one found on the Green Sheet. It is beautiful to be at one of those schools and listen to 3- and 4-year-olds reciting Bible passages, the Lord's Prayer, and the Apostles' Creed by heart.

Unfortunately, some congregations cave in to the pressures of the self-absorbed culture, and as a result are focusing less and less on the Word of God and more and more on surveys of what people think they want and need in a church. In other churches, many pastors and elders are being pressured by some within their congregations to do the same. Michael Horton, in his book, *Christless Christianity: The Alternative Gospel of the American Church,* writes,

> I think that the church in America today is so obsessed with being practical, relevant, helpful, successful, and perhaps even well-liked that it nearly mirrors the world itself. Aside from the packaging, there is nothing that cannot be found in most churches today that could not be satisfied by any number of secular programs and self-help groups.[4]

Some believe that in order to reach young people, the church needs to lighten up by meeting their felt needs and entertaining them. Many, including Horton, have found just the opposite to be the case. He writes,

> Increasingly, a younger generation is taking leadership that was raised on hype and hypocrisy and is weary of the narcissistic (i.e., "me-centered") orientation of their parents' generation. They are attracted to visions of salvation larger than the legalistic individualism of salvation-as-fire-insurance. Yet they are also fed up with the consumeristic individualism of salvation-as-personal-improvement. Instead, they are desperately craving authenticity and genuine transformation that produces true community, exhibiting loving acts that address the wider social and global crises of our day rather than the narrow jeremiads of yesteryear.[5]

Pastors and elders, this self-absorbed world needs more of the Word of God, not less. St. Paul's admonition to hold fast to the Word of God is as relevant today as the day he wrote it. "Now I would remind you, brothers, of the gospel I preached to you, which you received, in which you stand, and by which you are being saved, if you hold fast to the word I preached to you—unless you believed in vain" (1 Corinthians 15:1–2). Jesus said, "If anyone loves Me, he will keep My word, and My Father will love him, and We will come to him and make Our home with him. Whoever does not love Me does not keep My words" (John 14:23–24a). In the world, "it's all about me!" In the Church, it is all about God's Word!

FOR REFLECTION AND DISCUSSION

1. List examples of how Christians are becoming more and more conformed to the world.

2. How many members of your congregation have a "hatch (baptize), match (marry), and dispatch (bury)" understanding of the pastoral ministry? What can be done to change this view of the Church and its ministry?

3. Are there members of your congregation who recognize the need for their child(ren) to be baptized but fail to see the need to feed the faith created in Holy Baptism on a weekly basis? What are some things pastors and elders can do to change that?

4. How can elders assist the pastor(s) in teaching members of the congregation the importance of hearing the Word of God and partaking of the Sacrament on a weekly basis?

5. How can elders assist the pastor in handling the issue of couples living together before marriage? What are the issues involved and the goal of care for those in this situation?

6. What is the state of marriage and family in your congregation? How many of the families within your congregation have been affected by divorce?

7. How have sports affected attendance at weekly Divine Services and Bible classes in your congregation? What are some things that pastors and elders can do to address this?

8. What is the source of President Meyer's optimism concerning the future of The Lutheran Church—Missouri Synod?

9. What is Christian mediation and how is it done?

10. Where is the answer to the challenge of a self-absorbed culture to be found?

Working within One's Vocation

Chapter FIVE

For by the grace given to me I say to everyone among you not to think of himself more highly than he ought to think, but to think with sober judgment, each according to the measure of faith that God has assigned. For as in one body we have many members, and the members do not have all the same function, so we, though many, are one body in Christ, and individually members one of another.

—Romans 12:3–5

God is at work in His people through their various vocations. Far from being merely a career, a vocation is a calling—a station in life in which a person is given something to do. The vocations we are given in life are really gifts of God. For example, I did not choose the calling of being a son, but was given that role by God. Having been blessed by God with a wife and children, I was also given the calling to be a husband and father. God called me through the Church to be a pastor. In a similar way, elders are also called to work in the church, as they are not only asked to serve but also appointed by the congregation. These callings are labors of love. Gene Edward Veith Jr., who has written extensively about the doctrine of vocation, says:

The doctrine of vocation has to do with the mystery of individuality, how God creates each human being to be different from all of the rest and gives each a unique calling in every stage of life. Thus you have particular talents, which you are to understand are His gifts. You have a particular personality, with interests, likes, and dislikes that not everyone shares. Such is the plentitude of God's creation that no two people—or snowflakes or leaves or anything God has made—are exactly alike. Vocations are likewise unique, with no two people taking up exactly the same space in the family, the nation, the church, or the workplace. Finding your vocation, then, has to do, in part, with finding your God-given talents (what you can do) and your God-given personality (what fits the person you are).[1]

Pastors and elders bring different gifts in service to the Lord and His Church. Instead of attempting to get everyone to do the same thing, it is far better to use the talents and abilities of each person in a way that is in accord with their talents and that fits with who they are. For example, there are some elders who will tend to be good at speaking in front of people at voters' meetings while others find following up with members behind the scenes a better fit. Both public speaking and individual follow-up with members of the congregation are important tasks for elders. Likewise, different pastors will have different strengths and weaknesses relative to the different aspects of their vocation as pastors.

Matching the task with someone who has a talent for that task will be far more beneficial to the congregation than assigning a task to someone who is ill-equipped to carry it out. Veith explains it this way:

> In God's design, each person is to love his or her neighbors and to serve them with the gifts appropriate to each vocation. This means that I serve you with my talents, and you serve me with your talents. The result is a divine division of labor in which everyone is constantly giving and receiving in a vast interchange, a unity of diverse people in a social order whose substance and energy is love.
>
> I don't have to build my own house. Someone else builds it for me. Someone else has made my clothes. I depend on farmers, bakers, grocery store workers for my daily bread.[2]

It is important that a person assigned a particular task is qualified, prepared, and confident in his abilities to accomplish what he is given to do. In the Old Testament, we hear how Moses was not confident at all in his abilities to speak publicly.

Moses said to the LORD, "Oh my Lord, I am not eloquent, either in the past or since You have spoken to Your servant, but I am slow of speech and of tongue." Then the LORD said to him, "Who has made man's mouth? Who makes him mute, or deaf, or see-ing, or blind? Is it not I, the LORD? Now therefore go, and I will be with your mouth and teach you what you shall speak." But he said, "Oh, my Lord, please send someone else." Then the anger of the LORD was kindled against Moses and He said, "Is there not Aaron, your brother, the Levite? I know that he can speak well. Behold, he is coming out to meet you, and when he sees you, he will be glad in his heart. You shall speak to him and put the words in his mouth, and I will be with your mouth and with his mouth and will teach you both what to do. He shall speak for you to the people, and he shall be your mouth, and you shall be as God to him." (Exodus 4:10–16)

Aaron, unlike Moses, obviously had a gift for public speaking. He worked with Moses and assisted him in serving the people of God using the talents and abilities that God had given him in the area of public speaking. This does not mean that Moses didn't have to do anything or that God was replacing Moses with someone else. Moses was still called by God to lead the people of God out of Egypt.

A person's gifting can be improved—or even added to!—over time. As Moses carried out his vocation and gained experience in serving the Lord and leading the people he became more gifted, even at public speaking. As a pas-tor, I believe that I am a much better preacher now than I was when first called into the Office of the Holy Ministry. This is because I intentionally worked at becoming better at it, and still do. We all know pastors who do not have a nat-ural gift for public speaking, an obviously important component of preaching. This does not mean that they are not faithful and good pastors. Their strengths may lie in conducting individual visits with members of the congregation or in the comfort they bring to members dealing with illness or the death of loved ones. And yet, elders and pastors can assist one another in improving their skills by being honest about areas of their ministry that they can improve upon. They can also make continuing education opportunities available by which they can improve their skills in ministry.

When a pastor isn't doing some aspect of his vocation in the church or is conducting it poorly, a common first response is to seek his removal and find someone else. Take, for example, a pastor who is not visiting his people who are in the hospital or nursing homes and therefore is failing in his vocation of providing proper pastoral care for those in need. Instead of simply insisting on it being done, try to find out why this important aspect of pastoral care is not being done. Could it be that the pastor has a hard time with this aspect of his vocation? Pastors are asked to do a lot of things. Instead of assuming they should be great at all of them, assist them in order to improve in those areas of ministry that are in need of growth. This is far better than seeking to remove them from their call by forcing them to resign. Notice that God did not remove Moses from his call to lead the Israelites out of Egypt, even though He was angry with him. Instead God gave Moses someone who would help him in this task. Elders are called to assist the pastor in those weaker aspects of his vocational ministry in order to help him faithfully serve those entrusted to his care.

When asking elders to do something outside of their vocation, especially without training, we are setting them up to fail at a ministry that is intended to help. One year, a board of elders had set aside part of every meeting to make phone calls to members. Each elder was to go to a different area of the church and school, make some calls, and then after a period of time come back and discuss with one another their calls. For some, this worked out well, and they had some good discussions with members on the phone. Others spent the time staring at the phone or said that they would do it later.

Making a cold call is not a given vocation for some elders. Those who struggled with this but still made some calls had a hard time carrying on a conversation, leaving the member on the other end of the phone wondering what the call was all about. If the church had offered some training beforehand, perhaps these elders would have had more success in accomplishing this task. For others, it would have been better still to offer an alternative way of contacting members, like writing a personal note.

In assigning tasks on the board of elders, think in terms of who each elder is as a person. The personality style of each elder (referred to in Chapter 3) is one thing that you might want to take into consideration. For example, an elder with a doer personality will tend to be good at running an elder meeting effectively. Those elders with connector or charmer personality styles can be good at relating and forming a personal connection with people. Get them out and among the people of the congregation! An elder with a perfectionist personality style may help elders remain disciplined in accomplishing the tasks they have set out to do.

A proper understanding of vocation reminds us that God has called us into many different roles, and we each have a unique responsibility to fulfill His calling in each one. There was a missionary many years ago who was so focused on his call as a missionary that he neglected his wife and family. Although his son was struggling with drug addiction and there were other serious family issues, he told his wife that it was more important for him to be overseas and that she should stay home and take care of the family. This was a case where the pastor failed to realize that his call to be a father, for example, was just as important as his call to be a pastor.

Likewise, elders are not authorized to do certain tasks within the Church that pastors are given to do. Gene Edward Veith Jr. addresses this issue of authority in vocation when he writes:

> Different vocations have their own kinds of authority and spheres of action, and they operate under different rules. It would be the grossest immorality for someone to make perfect strangers take off their clothes and then cut their bodies open with a knife. But this is permissible and an act of love and service for someone who is carrying out the vocation of surgeon. Having sex is immoral outside of marriage, but it is a great good within the vocation of marriage.

> When someone injures us, our impulse is to take personal revenge, which is sharply forbidden by Scripture. Punishing crimes—whether this involves high-speed chases, shoot-outs, throwing someone in jail, or executing them—simply is not our vocation. This is, however, the vocation of police officers, judges, and the rest of the legal system.[3]

Just because an elder has the talents and abilities to do something that a pastor does doesn't mean he should. For example, an elder is likely capable to speak the Words of Institution over the elements of the bread and wine of Holy Communion. However, his vocation as elder is not one that has not been authorized by God through the Church to do it. "Our churches teach that no one should publicly teach in the Church, or administer the Sacraments, without a rightly ordered call."[4]

St. Paul reminds each of us "not to think of himself more highly than he ought to think, but to think with sober judgment, each according to the measure of faith that God has assigned" (Romans 12:3). Sometimes pastors get so caught up in their work that they think that they are indispensable. Elders need to help and support their pastors by reminding them of what they are called to do and what they are not called to do. If pastors try to do it all, they will eventually end up engaged in activities that take them away from what they were called and ordained to do as pastors. This happened in the Early Church, and the apostles took steps to correct it so that they could continue to devote themselves to the proper work of pastoral ministry.

> Now in these days when the disciples were increasing in number, a complaint by the Hellenists arose against the Hebrews because their widows were being neglected in the daily distribution. And the twelve summoned the full number of the disciples and said, "It is not right that we should give up preaching the word of God to serve tables. Therefore, brothers, pick out from among you seven men of good repute, full of the Spirit and of wisdom, whom we will appoint to this duty. But we will devote ourselves to prayer and to the ministry of the word." (Acts 6:1–4)

The apostles understood that they were not authorized to do everything in the Church, even if they could. It is why they appointed others to carry out the service of general care while they paid attention to pastoral care.

The apostle Paul refers to Christians as being like a body. Each part of the body has a different function, yet every part is connected to and dependent on another. When thinking about the body, think of how the head directs each part of the body to do what it is given to do. The eyes, mouth, ears, hands, and feet are all given different tasks to do. They cannot do these tasks independent of the head. When the connection between the head and the legs is severed as a result of an accident, the legs are paralyzed. They can do nothing, and this adversely affects the other parts of the body, handicapping them in regard to what they too are able to do. Without the head, the other parts of the body are useless. In the same way, the Church cannot do anything without Jesus, her head.

> [Jesus] is the image of the invisible God, the firstborn of all creation. For by Him all things were created, in heaven and on earth, visible and invisible, whether thrones or dominions or rulers or authorities—all things were created through Him and for Him. And He is before all things, and in Him all things hold together. And He is the head of the body, the church. (Colossians 1:15–18a)

Both pastors and elders need to remember that Jesus is the head of the Church and that makes the Church different from merely human institutions. Although pastors and elders bring different gifts in service to the Lord and His Church, each gift is to be used exclusively at the direction of Christ, the head. Os Guinness in his book *Dining with the Devil* warns about this when he writes:

> If Jesus Christ is true, the church is more than just another human institution. He alone is her head. He is the sole source and single goal. His grace uniquely is her effective principle. What moves her is not finally interchangeable with the dynamics of even the closest of sister institutions. When the best of modern insights and tools are in full swing, there should always be a remainder, an irreducible character that is more than the sum of all the human, the natural, and the organizational.

> If Jesus Christ is the head of the church and hence the source and goal of its entire life, true growth is only possible in obedience to him. Conversely, if the church becomes detached from Jesus Christ and his word, it cannot truly grow however active and successful it may seem to be. However spectacular its development, it will prove disappointing in the end. However celebrated

its progress, it will prove ultimately a falling away. The authentic movements in the church are those that are set in motion by God's decisive authority, especially the decisive authority of grace.[5]

Jesus, as the head of the Church, directs our work within our given vocations so that we act in accord with His Word. By the Holy Spirit working through the Word of God and by the Lord's very body and blood streaming through our veins as the body of Christ, we are enlivened, nurtured, and strengthened for service in our given vocations. St. Paul puts it this way:

> For the body does not consist of one member but of many. If the foot should say, "Because I am not a hand, I do not belong to the body," that would not make it any less a part of the body. And if the ear should say, "Because I am not an eye, I do not belong to the body," that would not make it any less a part of the body. If the whole body were an eye, where would be the sense of hearing? If the whole body were an ear, where would be the sense of smell? But as it is, God arranged the members in the body, each one of them, as He chose. If all were a single member, where would the body be? As it is, there are many parts, yet one body.

> The eye cannot say to the hand, "I have no need of you," nor again the head to the feet, "I have no need of you." On the contrary, the parts of the body that seem to be weaker are indispensable, and on those parts of the body that we think less honorable we bestow the greater honor, and our unpresentable parts are treated with greater modesty, which our more presentable parts do not require. But God has so composed the body, giving greater honor to the part that lacked it, that there may be no division in the body, but that the members may have the same care for one another. If one member suffers, all suffer together; if one member is honored, all rejoice together.

> Now you are the body of Christ, and individually members of it. And God has appointed in the church first apostles, second prophets, third teachers, then miracles, then gifts of healing, helping, administrating, and various kinds of tongues. Are all

apostles? Are all prophets? Are all teachers? Do all work miracles? Do all possess gifts of healing? Do all speak in tongues? Do all interpret? But earnestly desire the higher gifts. (1 Corinthians 12:12–31)

Pastors and elders have unique gifts, talents, and abilities that they have been called to use in their care for the Church and one another. Only when working within their given vocations and under Christ as their head will they accomplish what God has given them together to do in service to Him and His Church!

FOR REFLECTION AND DISCUSSION

1. Why is it important to remember that Jesus is the head of the Church, and what does that mean?

2. What is a vocation?

3. What does it mean to work within one's vocation? Why is working within one's vocation important?

4. At an elder meeting, ask each elder and the pastor to describe what he has been called by God to do in life. What are those things?

5. At the same meeting, ask each elder and the pastor to identify three strengths and three growth areas of what he has been called to do as an elder or pastor. What are those strength and growth areas?

6. Based on strengths and growth areas identified above, would some elders be better suited for a different vocation within the board of elders?

7. What are the benefits of identifying the various vocations that people have in the congregation?

8. Is the pastor involved in some vocations within the church that are taking him away from his vocation of Word and Sacrament ministry? If he is, who would be more suited to take on those tasks?

ACCOUNTABLE TO GOD THROUGH ONE ANOTHER

Let us therefore strive to enter that rest, so that no one may fall by the same sort of disobedience. For the word of God is living and active, sharper than any two-edged sword, piercing to the division of soul and of spirit, of joints and of marrow, and discerning the thoughts and intentions of the heart. And no creature is hidden from His sight, but all are naked and exposed to the eyes of Him to whom we must give an account.

—Hebrews 4:11–13

A woman with her two children wanted to ask a pastor a question. While she was talking to the pastor her little boy started hitting her young daughter. She told him to stop it. Instead of stopping, he kept hitting his sister. Again the mother told him to stop it. This happened several times, and each time the mother threatened the little boy with punishment. After no less than five threats and just as many warnings she finally told her daughter to just run so that her son wouldn't hit her anymore.

There was no punishment for the son, as was promised. He was not held accountable for his misbehavior. The mother didn't mean what she said. Her deeds didn't match her words. Perhaps without intending to, this mother taught her little boy that he didn't need to listen to her and that there are no consequences for wrongdoing. The mother didn't use the authority she was given as a parent to discipline her child, and as a result the son had no respect for her authority. The daughter in this incident was taught something, too. She was taught, when facing conflict, run!

The above incident is an example of one in authority failing to hold someone accountable for misbehavior. It is also an example of a general lack of respect for authority. This lack of respect for authority and the failure to recognize how we are accountable toward each other is common in our culture of today, and in the church. We seem to have forgotten—or maybe we never learned—that "Whoever resists the authorities resists what God has appointed, and those who resist will incur judgment" (Romans 13:2).

"Honor your father and mother. *What does this mean?* We should fear and love God so that we do not despise or anger our parents and other authorities, but honor them, serve, and obey them, love and cherish them" (Small Catechism, Fourth Commandment). Who are "parents and other authorities"? The Catechism states: "Parents are fathers, mothers, and guardians; other authorities are all those whom God has placed over us at home, in government, at school, at the place where we work, and in the church" (Small Catechism, Christian Questions, 48).

In their first meeting after he had received a call to serve a particular congregation, a pastor said to his board of elders, "I just want you to know that I am accountable to God, and not to you." While it is true that a pastor is accountable to God, that doesn't happen apart from certain means outside of the pastor himself. Even the pastor's call to serve the congregation teaches that fact. A pastor does not simply decide that he is going to serve a particular church. He is called by God through the Church to serve a particular congregation. He is also accountable to God through the Church. This means that the congregation does have the authority to discipline a pastor if he is not acting in accord with the Lord's Word or not doing what he has been called and ordained by God to do. Peter C. Bender writes,

> His ordination vows also require him to do the work of ministry, to keep the seal of the confessional absolute, and to adorn the Office of the Public Ministry with a holy life.
>
> A minister is called by God through the church. He is also removed by God through the church, if he (1) persistently adheres to false teaching, (2) continually fails or is unable to do the work of his office, or (3) dishonors his office through a manifest immoral life.[1]

Both pastor and congregation are held accountable to God through one another by means of God's Word. In the Divine Service the pastor says to the people this salutation, "The Lord be with you." The people respond by saying, "And also with you" or "And with your spirit" (*LSB*, p. 156). In this seemingly routine give-and-take, the pastor and fellow members of the Body of Christ are actually holding one another accountable to the Lord, who is present among them. In the salutation, the congregation is reminded that God comes to them in and through His authoritative Word, which the pastor preaches. The pastor is reminded of the presence of God and also of his ordination vow to not go beyond his authority and say only what the Lord says.

Any attempt to establish one's freedom from accountability is an attempt to usurp the authority of the Word of God. This is futile, and yet it happens all the time. So how did we get here? In the end, it has to do with what was talked about at the beginning, namely, the question of who is in charge. If authority lies within each individual instead of it being a commodity given to us by God, then people should just be allowed to do whatever they want. It is why, for many, the definition of love is to bless whatever anyone wants to do. As a consequence of such a twisted truth, it is considered unloving and intolerant to say that there are those who are wrong and that they need to repent. It is considered even worse if there are attempts to implement consequences for those who have done wrong.

The blessing of forgiveness is that instead of the sin remaining within us, it is removed. The goal of holding people accountable for what they have done wrong is the forgiveness of sins, and forgiveness is far better than futile attempts to minimize wrongdoing, or to pretend that it didn't happen. Among our leaders—even pastors and elders—we rarely hear genuine apologies, but often hear mere expressions of sorrow if someone was offended by something that was said or done. This is in reality a subtle way of denying responsibility for the wrongdoing. This is not genuine repentance. In addition, instead of offering forgiveness when someone is truly repentant, the wrong committed is at times minimized by saying, "That's okay." Sin is never okay. To be held accountable is to recognize the reality of sin and its consequences. Genuine repentance is to be met not by "That's okay," but by the words, "I forgive you."

This is why holding one another accountable is so important, though the discipline associated with it may seem at times unloving! The writer to the Hebrews reminds us:

> It is for discipline that you have to endure. God is treating you as sons. For what son is there whom the father does not discipline? If you are left without discipline, in which all have participated, then you are illegitimate children and not sons. Besides this, we have had earthly fathers who disciplined us and we respected them. Shall we not much more be subject to the Father of spirits and live? For they disciplined us for a short time as it seemed best to them, but He disciplines us for our good, that we may share His holiness. For the moment all discipline seems painful rather than pleasant, but later yields the peaceful fruit of righteousness to those who have been trained by it. (Hebrews 12:7–11)

Discipline in the Church is done for the good of all. Far from being unloving, it is, in fact, the loving practice of pastors and elders in their care for the Church and one another. And yet, like the ultimately unloving lack of discipline illustrated by the mom and her two children in the opening of this chapter, there is also a general lack of discipline in the Church. The fact that excommunications are almost unheard of either means that people sin less today than they did in the past or there is a failure to discipline in the Church. It is obviously the latter. The failure of pastors and elders to use the authority given by God through the Church to discipline those entrusted to their care has led to a general disrespect of that authority. Like the little boy that kept hitting his sister, there are those who don't think that God really means what He says in His Word. As a result, they don't believe that there are dire and eternal consequences to sin.

Pastors and elders are those whom God has authorized to practice discipline within the Church. If they don't practice disciplining those who sin, the people sinning will falsely think that there are no consequences to sin and that God simply overlooks it. The apostle Paul warns against such callous disregard of the consequences of sin when he says, "For the wrath of God is revealed from heaven against all ungodliness and unrighteousness of men, who by their unrighteousness suppress the truth" (Romans 1:18). When it comes to dealing with sin and conflict in the Church, pastors and elders seem to have taken the advice given to the little girl by her mother: run!

On the front of some pulpits there is a carving of an open Bible with a sword lying on it, illustrating that "the word of God is living and active, sharper than any two-edged sword" (Hebrews 4:12). Pastors, in their preaching and pastoral care in the Church, are to proclaim both the judgment of God and His forgiveness that comes in and through Jesus Christ. Elders are to do the same as they assist the pastor in caring for fellow members of the Body of Christ.

The purpose of proclaiming the Lord's judgment pertaining to sin is to expose sin and to bring those who are sinning to repentance so that they look to Jesus Christ for forgiveness and new life. The apostle Peter shows how this is done in a sermon from the Book of Acts.

> Let all the house of Israel therefore know for certain that God has made Him both Lord and Christ, this Jesus whom you crucified.
>
> Now when they heard this they were cut to the heart, and said to Peter and the rest of the apostles, "Brothers, what shall we do?" And Peter said to them, "Repent and be baptized every one of you in the name of Jesus Christ for the forgiveness of your sins, and you will receive the gift of the Holy Spirit. For the promise is for you and for your children and for all who are far off, everyone whom the Lord our God calls to Himself." And with many other words he bore witness and continued to exhort them, saying, "Save yourselves from this crooked generation." So those who received his word were baptized, and there were added that day about three thousand souls. And they devoted themselves to the apostles' teaching and fellowship, to the breaking of bread and the prayers. (Acts 2:36–42)

Many believe that proclaiming the judgment of God on sin will adversely affect numerical growth in the Church. So instead of condemning it, many pastors and elders overlook sin out of fear that those sinning will leave the Church.[2] When Peter speaks the truth in love, as in his sermon above, notice that instead of decline, there is great growth in the church!

Pastors and elders need to hold one another and fellow members of the

Body of Christ accountable to the whole counsel of God, both the Law and the Gospel, in their care for the Church and one another. In the end, it is about trusting in the authority of the Word of God. "All flesh is like grass and all its glory like the flower of the grass. The grass withers, and the flower falls, but the word of the Lord remains forever" (1 Peter 1:24–25).

FOR REFLECTION AND DISCUSSION

1. In what ways are pastors and elders accountable to one another? Why?

2. Why is it so difficult to practice discipline within the Church?

3. How does a failure to practice discipline within the Church lead to a general disrespect of authority within the Church?

4. Why is it so difficult to confront someone when he or she is sinning?

5. Look at the apostle Peter's entire sermon in Acts chapter two. Does he mince words when it comes to condemning sin?

6. What is the problem with overlooking unrepentant sin in the congregation?

7. How can pastors and elders do a better job of supporting one another when having to confront those who are unrepentant sinners?

CONCLUSION

Jesus said, "I am the Alpha and Omega, the first and the last, the beginning and the end" (Revelation 22:13). Everything begins and ends with Jesus, the Lord of heaven and earth. Throughout this book, pastors and elders have been deliberately and carefully drawn to Jesus to be equipped for their service to the Lord and His Church. Jesus is the One who not only directs what work is to be done, but works in and through those who confess Him in what they say and do. Jesus forges trust between elders and pastors as they live together in the way of repentance and the forgiveness of sins. Jesus gives pastors and elders different talents, abilities, wisdom, and skills, that each may work together and grow in their appreciation of how God works within multiple vocations to benefit His Church. The way of Jesus' genuine love and care assists pastors and elders in being held accountable to God through one another—a thing once intimidating, but now something no longer to be feared. And while the task of bringing Jesus' Gospel to a self-absorbed culture may at times seem overwhelming, God has promised that His Word will not return empty.

> For as the rain and the snow come down from heaven and do not return there but water the earth, making it bring forth and sprout, giving seed to the sower and bread to the eater, so shall My word be that goes out from My mouth; it shall not return to me empty, but it shall accomplish that which I purpose, and shall succeed in the thing for which I sent it. (Isaiah 55:10–11)

"Therefore, my beloved brothers, be steadfast, immovable, always abounding in the work of the Lord, knowing that in the Lord your labor is not in vain" (1 Corinthians 15:58).

The following is an example of the Green Sheet" mentioned in Chapter 2. It is printed landscape on one sheet of 8 ½ x 11 paper, double-sided, and inserted in the bulletin every week.

Appendix A

The Sixteenth Sunday after Pentecost
October 2, 2011

Introit

Ps. 118:22–24; antiphon: Ps. 118:1

Oh give thanks to the Lord, for | he is good;*

for his steadfast love endures for- | ever!

The stone that the builders re- | jected*

has become the | cornerstone.

This is the Lord's | doing;*

it is marvelous | in our eyes.

This is the day that the | Lord has made;*

let us rejoice and be | glad in it.

Glory be to the Father and | to the Son*

and to the Holy | Spirit;

as it was in the be- | ginning,*

is now, and will be forever. | Amen.

Oh give thanks to the Lord, for | he is good;*

for his steadfast love endures for- | ever!

Collect

Gracious God, You gave Your Son into the hands of sinful men who killed Him. Forgive us when we reject Your unfailing love, and grant us the fullness of Your salvation; through Jesus Christ, Your Son, our Lord, who lives and reigns with You and the Holy Spirit, one God, now and forever.

Gradual

He will command his angels con- | cerning you*

to guard you in | all your ways.

Bless the Lord, | O my soul,*

and all that is within me, bless his | holy name!

Learn by Heart: The First Article (paragraphs 1–2)

LSB # 322

Readings for Next Sunday: Isaiah 25:6–9; Philippians 4:4–13; Matthew 22:1–14

[handwritten notes: Put it in the email ... Time & Day issues etc ... to get ready for the next Sunday]

83

The Green Sheet

CONGREGATION AT PRAYER AND DEVOTIONS FOR THE WEEK

INVOCATION

INTROIT (front page)

LEARN BY HEART: Bible Verse and Catechism (front page)

MEDITATION: *Portals of Prayer* / Devotion

DAILY READINGS: *Treasures of Daily Prayer*

Sun: Deut. 3:1–29; Matt. 7:1–12

Mon: Deut. 4:1–20; Matt. 7:13–29

Tues: Deut. 4:21–40; Matt. 8:1–17

Wed: Deut. 5:1–21; Matt. 8:18–34

Thurs: Deut. 5:22–6:9; Matt. 9:1–17

Fri: Deut. 6:10–25; Matt. 9:1–18

Sat: Deut. 7:1–19; Matt. 10:1–23

IN OUR PRAYERS THIS WEEK: *we don't list the reasons*

- Clair, stepfather of Lana, ALS
- Barb, recovering after surgery
- Paul, cancer treatment
- Lynn, cancer
- Paula, sister of Corinne, cancer
- Jim, father of Andy, myeloma cancer
- Those currently serving our country in the military: Timothy, Brian, Harvey, Michael, Robert, Joey, Robert, Andrew, and Justin
- Ruth, friend of Mike, cancer
- Holly, undergoing tests

- Esther, ill
- Helen, mother of Carla, undergoing tests
- Stephanie, recovering after an accident
- Addison, newborn daughter of Chad & Tara, hospitalized
- Jasmine, friend of Billy & Catherine, hospitalized
- Tammy, friend of Kathy, cancer
- Tom, son of Emily, undergoing cancer treatment

HYMN OF THE WEEK "The God of Abraham Praise" *LSB # 798*

COLLECT (front page)

APOSTLES' CREED

LORD'S PRAYER

BENEDICTION

The following are sample elder letters. The first two letters are addressed to someone who has been inactive. The others are sample letters that elders might send out every Advent and Lent.

I was glad when they said to me,
"Let us go to the house of the LORD!"

—Psalm 122:1

Dear Member of *(your church name)*,

It is with great sadness that we note that you have not been regularly worshiping with us at *(your church name)* for quite some time. If there is something that we have done or not done that has led you away, please let us know so that we might repent and reconcile with you. We're not perfect at *(your church name)*, and we know that we may have inadvertently said or done something that has lead you away from worshiping with us. If that is the case, we ask for your forgiveness.

We genuinely want you to join with us at *(your church name)* in receiving the grace of God in Jesus Christ every Sunday in the Divine Service. Be assured that our Lord who has promised to be wherever two or three are gathered in His name will be here to bless you with all the treasures of heaven. As an elder, I along with our pastors have no agenda except to serve you with the Gospel of Jesus Christ in both word and deed.

Please let us know if you plan to return to us, and know that it is our heartfelt prayer that you do. You can contact me by phone at *(phone number)* or by e-mail at *(e-mail address)*. If I don't hear from you soon, I will follow up with a call. We hope to see you soon!

In Christ,

Member of the Board of Elders
(your church name)

Sample Letters

Dear *(name)*,

We have missed seeing you at God's house these past weeks and are writing you this brief note to let you know. (Of course, there is always the possibility that we simply overlooked you in the crowd—and if that is the case, accept our apologies. Also remind us of it.)

When a brother or sister is absent from the services, it could be a matter of sickness, work, or vacation that has legitimately kept him away. When there is a reason for a member's absence, we—the pastor and board of elders—like to know. It is our duty and privilege to care about, and care for, all the members of the congregation. You are precious to us, as you are to the Lord Himself.

In case there is sickness or hardship in the family, we especially want to know so that we can offer our help and our prayers. And we would urge you to contact the pastor immediately to discuss the matter with him.

Of course, it is always possible for God's children to lose some of their zeal to hear God's Word preached, to worship their loving God, and to fellowship with the other saints. It is so easy for the cares, the pleasures, the busy-ness of life itself to interfere with heart and soul activities. Where this is the case, we can only recommend the remedial action of returning at once to the house of God to hear His Word and receive the Sacrament, which alone can make one's faith and love burn hot again.

We hope that nothing of a serious matter—either physical or spiritual—has developed in your life to keep you from exercising your rights and privileges as a member of *(your church name)* congregation. We are looking forward to enjoying your fellowship in the near future.

> Blessed . . . are those who hear the
> word of God and keep it! (Luke 11:28)

Yours in the Service of Our Savior,

Chairman of the Board Elders   Pastor

Dear Member of *(your church name),*

The seasons of Advent and Christmas are upon us once again. As your elder, I thought this an especially appropriate time to write to you in order to encourage you in the faith. Unfortunately, this can be a very hectic time of year as we attempt to meet everyone's expectations of us. Often, we end up wearing ourselves out running after the things of this world, with little energy left for our Lord and one another.

The message of Advent and Christmas is that our Lord comes to bring us together with Him and one another through His Word and Sacrament. Real life and peace are not found in the things of this world but in our Lord Jesus Christ and the life He has given us to live together. Enclosed you will find a brochure detailing all the dates and times of services through the Epiphany of our Lord. We will also be handing out more at church for you to use as invitations for others to join us at *(your church name).*

I am here to assist the pastors in serving you, so if I can be of help, or, if you have any questions or concerns, please feel free to give me a call. I look forward to receiving the Lord's Gospel gifts with you this Advent and Christmas season.

In Christ,

Member of the Board of Elders
(your church name)

Sample Letters

Dear Member of *(your church name),*

The Lord calls His people to return. "The time is fulfilled, and the kingdom of God is at hand; repent and believe in the gospel" (Mark 1:15). These words of Jesus, at the start of His public ministry, come upon His return to Galilee after forty days of fasting and His temptation in the desert. We will also hear during this upcoming Lent that we are made of dust and to dust we shall return (Genesis 3:19). These godly and loving reminders tell us that He made us, it is His work, we are His, and He wants us to be with Him. Our Lord's words cause us to turn, repent, to return.

Some of us may be feeling as if we are wandering in the wilderness of employment, finances, family matters, health, or other serious concerns at this time. And we perhaps may not always care for the serious side of Lent. The forty days of Lent, however, do not leave us alone on the ash heap. Beginning with Ash Wednesday, we are lead to a triumphant Easter Day and our own Baptism into Christ. Lent is a serious matter. It's about death and life, sin and forgiveness, grace and mercy, through the Word made flesh. "With His stripes we are healed" (Isaiah 53:5).

Each Sunday in Lent is a celebration. Worship at *(your church name)* echoes Christ's victory over death. Sunday, *(date),* is also a special day of celebration for our congregation. The *(your church name)* Showcase is opportunity to rejoice and enjoy the works of the Lord through the members of *(your church name).* Our heavenly Father can truly do amazing things with dust. Please join us at noon that day for what promises to be a fun-filled afternoon of making known the love of Christ.

As your elder, I encourage you to take advantage of the numerous worship opportunities at *(your church name)* this Lententide as our Lord calls and comes to us. Enclosed please find a brochure detailing the dates and times of services from Ash Wednesday through Holy Week and Easter. More of these brochures will be available at church for you to use as invitations for others to join us at *(your church name).*

If you have not been to *(your church name)* in a while, please return as our Lord calls. It is wonderful to see many members return weekly to the celebration of Christ's gifts. This year, also consider returning for Wednesday Lenten services *(insert time[s])* and/or return to one or more of the weekly Bible studies offered at *(your church name).*

Elders are to assist the pastors in serving the members of *(your church name).* If I can be of help, or if you have any questions or concerns, please feel free to call. I look forward to joining you this Lenten season at *(your church name),* departing to make known the love of Christ, and returning often to receive all of the gifts Christ has to offer.

In Christ,

Member of Board of Elders
(your church name)

Dear Member of *(your church name),*

The season of Lent is approaching once again. Lent is that time in the Church Year in which we are disciplined to deplore our sin in repentance and to look in faith to Christ Jesus, the Lamb of God who takes away the sins of the world. As your elder, I encourage you to be faithful in worship both on Sundays and also as we gather together for the midweek Lenten services on Wednesdays. Please note that following the 10 a.m. and 6:30 p.m. midweek Lenten services, you are invited to join fellow members of *(your church name)* for a soup luncheon or dinner. This is a nice opportunity to enjoy the company of one another.

Enclosed is a brochure detailing all the dates and times of services through Easter Sunday. We will also be handing out more at church for you to use as invitations for others to join us at *(your church name).* The words of the following hymn are a fitting prayer for us as we enter another Lenten season:

> On my heart imprint Your image, Blessed Jesus, King of grace,
> That life's riches, cares, and pleasures Never may Your work erase;
> Let the clear inscription be: Jesus, crucified for me,
> Is my life, my hope's foundation, And my glory and salvation!"
>
> —"On My Heart Imprint Your Image" (*LSB* 422)

If I can be of any assistance to you, please feel free to call me. I look forward to seeing you in church!

In Christ,

Member of Board of Elders
(your church name)

Sample Letters

Sample Elder Agenda

BOARD OF ELDERS MEETNG
(YOUR CHURCH NAME)

VISION: Making Known the Love of Christ

MISSION: (Your church name) is dedicated to the proclamation of the Gospel of Jesus Christ within and through its church and school.

THE BOARD OF ELDE RS: Assist pastors in all matters pertaining to the spiritual welfare of the congregation.

AGENDA

Date/Time/Place

- ☐ Opening devotion (Pastor)

- ☐ Minutes of last meeting

- ☐ Chairman's report

- ☐ Membership changes

- ☐ List and discuss changes

- ☐ Reports of Committees/recommendations

  - Worship

  - Ushers

  - Personnel Committee

  - Membership spiritual care—calls, highlights, tips

- ☐ Old business

- ☐ New business

- ☐ Study of Scripture and Lutheran Confessions

- ☐ Closing devotion (Pastor)

Goals for the Board of Elders

- Make visits and calls to all members of (your church name)—Minimum of three each month.
- Assist with updating church records (in conjunction with calls).
- Attend weekly Divine Service, Advent, Lenten services, and weekly Bible study
- Attend each Board meeting. Notify the church office when unable to attend and follow up with Board Chairman after missed meeting to address any action items.
- Promote (your church name) and educate membership concerning (your church name)'s vision and mission.
- Personal support for pastor(s) including weekly pre-service devotion.
- Become familiar with (your church name) Constitution, Employee Handbook, Position Description Booklet, and School Student/Parent Handbook.

To: Board of Elders

From: Pastor—May/June Report

Date:

In Nomine Jesu

Worship

☐ List attendance and other information relative to worship

Teaching

☐ List all classes

Pastoral Care

☐ List hospital, shut-in, and pastoral care visits and appointments

☐ List pre-marriage meetings with couples

Baptisms

☐ List the names of those baptized and dates of Baptisms

Other New Members

☐ List the names of other new members, dates they were received, and how they became members (e.g., adult Baptism, adult confirmation, transfer, profession of faith)

Funerals

☐ List names and dates of funerals

Weddings and Anniversary Services

☐ List names of those married or celebrating their marriage with anniversary services, along with the dates of weddings and anniversary services

New Members

☐ List names of new members and dates they were received

Membership

☐ List current baptized membership

☐ List current communicant membership

Administrative

☐ List all administrative tasks

Soli Deo Gloria

Sample Pastor Report

THE FIVE MOST PRESSING NEEDS OF PASTORS

Dr. Rev. Richard Koehneke identifies the five most pressing needs of pastors in the opening paragraphs of his essay. Rev. Koehneke has served for 38 years in full-time pastoral ministry, recently retiring in 2009 as senior pastor of Holy Cross in Fort Wayne, Indiana (1993–2009). His essay summarizes research he conducted for Concordia Theological Seminary early in 2010.

In January 2010, President Dean Wenthe of our Fort Wayne seminary and I agreed that I would try to identify the most pressing needs of pastors and assist the seminary to renew and encourage pastors for ministry and mission.

In my 38 years in full-time parish pastoral ministry (1971–2009) God saw fit to provide me with a rich variety of opportunities to be involved in the lifelong process of pastoral formation. I served on the LCMS Commission on Ministerial Growth and Support for nine years (2001–2010) and as one of the original facilitators in the PALS (Post-Seminary Applied Learning and Support) initiative of the LCMS, working in a collegial support group with six pastors in their first three years of ministry. I served as a mentor pastor in the Pastoral Leadership Institute from 2002–2009. It was my privilege to supervise ten vicars during my years in ministry (nine in New Jersey, one in Fort Wayne). During my sixteen years at Holy Cross, Fort Wayne, I supervised about 30 "field workers" during their first two years at the seminary.

I have some ideas about the most pressing needs of pastors, both from my own experience and from my interactions with brother pastors over the years. But I did not want to import my biases to the research President Wenthe and I had agreed I would carry out.

I had interactions—in person, on the telephone, and by email—with 55 persons (30 parish pastors, 14 district presidents, and 11 others) from February through April of 2010. Reviewing these responses, five needs began to emerge as high-priority items among all my research partners.

THE FIVE MOST PRESSING NEEDS OF PASTORS:

1. Safe places and people with whom a pastor can be transparent, express problems and needs, and find help and encouragement to carry on

Pastors need to know that asking for help is not a sign of weakness and illness, but strength and health. Pastors frequently feel isolated, inadequate, and insecure. We encourage others to ask for help, and often we are the ones to give it, but we are reluctant to ask for help ourselves. There is sometimes a critical and competitive spirit between and among pastors that makes it difficult to ask a brother pastor for help with personal problems and needs. Circuit counselors may or may not have the confidence of pastors in the circuit. District presidents acknowledge that they cannot provide a completely safe place from the pastor's perspective, since they are supervisors of the pastor's life and doctrine—a fact that does not always promote transparency in communication of problems and needs. Districts have ministerial health committees; therapists may be available through the district president; and the Concordia Health Plan includes the Employee Assistance Program, all of which are good and helpful. But there is still a missing component in the synodical system: a true "pastor to the pastor." When there are no safe places and people for the pastor to go for help, he may develop a pattern of rationalization, making excuses, blaming, denial, and even deception—thus doing great harm to himself, his marriage, his family, his ministry, and those he serves. When pastors are able and willing to ask for help before a problem degenerates into a crisis, the lives of many are helped, blessed, and saved.

Pastor Needs

2. A faithful, disciplined personal life of prayer and devotion

You cannot give what you do not have. You can "run on fumes" for only so long before you come to a dead stop. Pastors can become so busy searching the Scriptures for their next sermon or Bible class that they do not have time to sit at the feet of Jesus and listen to His teaching, simply for the sake of the relationship with Him, without any other agenda or task to be accomplished. Prayer life can become rushed and superficial until it becomes nearly nonexistent. In such a situation, there is a clear and present danger of spiritual burnout, when the pastor simply has nothing left. There is the (perhaps greater) danger of worldly and carnal success, when the pastor is operating in the power of the flesh, not the strength of the Spirit, and things seem to be going well, but God is neither glorified nor pleased. In between lies the danger of the pastor's own faith being in a consistently weakened condition, unable to meet the challenges and seize the opportunities of ministry. On the other hand, when the pastor is taking care of his own faith and his personal relationship with the Lord, there is a resilience, a calmness, even a buoyancy to his ministry that cannot have its source in anyone but Christ.

3. Learning to lead by team-building, equipping, and mobilizing

"If you want a job done right, do it yourself!" This motto, while it may possess some truth, also contains the seeds of workaholism, loneliness, and diminishing ministry. Many pastors equate working hard with working alone. Either because of the need to prove themselves worthy of their call (and salary), or because of a lack of trust of others, they try to do the work of ministry pretty much on their own, asking the people to watch and pray (if that) while they wrestle with the demons and demands that are always present in pastoral ministry. Such an attitude and approach contradict the clear wisdom and counsel of Scripture and the pattern of ministry of our Lord Himself. Jesus taught His disciples so that they could go and make disciples. On the mountain in Galilee when Jesus met the disciples after His resurrection, He did NOT say, "Since all authority in heaven and earth has been given to me, I will go and make disciples, and you will watch me work!" When the pastor believes (sincerely and with good motives, to be sure) that the work of ministry rests squarely and exclusively on his shoulders, he unintentionally limits the amount of ministry to whatever is the maximum that he can do by himself. Team-building, equipping, and mobilizing are necessary not only in the larger, multi-staffmember congregation, but also in the smaller congregation in which the ministry team may consist of the pastor and various members of the congregation. When the properly equipped people of God are entrusted with the work of God appropriate to their gifts and spiritual maturity (Romans 12, 1 Corinthians 12, Ephesians 4), dynamic spiritual energy is released for the work of the gospel.

4. Help in reaching our postmodern, post-church culture with the Gospel

Many of the people around us not only are apathetic to the work of the church, they actually resent the church and are hostile to those who proclaim the Word of God. They see the church, and pastors in particular, as irrelevant, narrow-minded, greedy, hypocritical, homophobic, conflicted—and that's just for starters. When they see us coming, they either put up their guard or run screaming in the opposite direction. It is difficult for pastors who have been prepared and equipped for ministry in the "churched" and "modern" culture to do ministry and mission in such a time as this. Pastors are accustomed to teaching and preaching, and in some cases defending the faith against attack, but we are not so proficient at the invitational style of communication that is most helpful and effective when we are in contact with the children of this world in the 21st century. This does not mean watering down our preaching and teaching, but it does mean paying attention to interpersonal conversations and relationships in the daily business and commerce of everyday life. Pastors have much wisdom to share, and the great Good News of Christ to proclaim, but if no one is listening, no good is accomplished. We may speak in the tongues of men and angels, but if we are not motivated by love, we sound to the hearers like a noisy gong or clanging cymbal. No one likes to listen to that sort of sound for very long. When people sense that we care, that we really have their best interests at heart, that we are willing to listen and clarify before responding, that we are willing to invest ourselves in them and their

Pastor Needs

situation, that we will not stop loving and caring no matter what—great things can happen, and there is joy in heaven over every lost sinner who repents and is saved.

5. Healthy marriage and family, and healthy balance and boundaries

Pastors' marriages and families are under attack and assault. That fact is nothing new, but the attacks seem to be coming from a wider array of sources, not the least of which is the revolution in information technology. The children of pastors are subject to a barrage of images and information unimaginable to previous generations. Marriages are under stress as children act out and rebel. Internet addictions and obsessions, including (but not limited to) pornography, can infect and corrupt the heart of the pastor, his wife, and his children. The work of ministry is so wide-ranging and diverse that a pastor could be saying "yes" 24 hours a day, 7 days a week, and still be nowhere near getting the job done. We need "knowledge and depth of insight to discern what is best" (Philippians 1), to decide what really matters and to focus our best efforts and energy on that. As someone has said, we need to schedule our priorities, not prioritize our schedule. Ministry is not ordinarily a choice between good and evil (thank God!) but making daily choices between good, better and best. There are few things more wonderful to behold (and to be) than a pastor who is concentrating his energy and attention on developing and using his best gifts to do his best work in the most important areas of the ministry in which God has placed him. And there are few things in this world that are more lovely and delightful than a pastor's marriage and family marked by deep respect, authentic joy, and the love that comes as the fruit of the Spirit into a heart and home filled with faith in Christ.

—From Doxology: The Lutheran Center for Spiritual Care and Counsel, www.doxology.us, "Pastoral Notes," newsletter 3, no. 3 (November 2010).

SAMPLE JOB DESCRIPTION—
BOARD OF ELDERS

ACCOUNTABLE TO: _____

PURPOSE: To oversee the spiritual life of the congregation and its individual members.

DUTIES AND RESPONSIBILITIES:

These guidelines are as intended by the congregation's constitution and the bylaws.

1. The Board of Elders shall have authority and responsibility for the spiritual welfare and activities of the congregational members, individually and corporately.

2. The chairman of the Board of Elders shall preside at all meetings of the Board of Elders.

    a. The chairman shall appoint a secretary to record the minutes.

    b. The chairman shall appoint one elder to serve as an advisor on, at a minimum, each of the following committees: Worship, Board of Christian Education, Ushers, Social ministry, New Member Ministry, Youth and Health Ministry. Other committee assignments may be made to other ongoing and ad hoc committees in the congregation including, but not limited to, Assimilation, Public Relations and Sanctity of Life.

    c. The chairman will report the recommendations of the Board of Elders to the church council and the voters assembly.

    d. The chairman may call special meetings of the Board of Elders.

3. The Board of Elders shall meet once a month, except that up to twice per year they may be cancelled with consent of the pastor(s).

4. The Board of Elders shall consist of not less than **xxx** nor more than **xxx** geographic elders, not including the chairman, such number to be established from time to time by the voter's assembly. While the entire Board of Elders is responsible for the spiritual welfare and activities of the congregation, both individually and corporately, as a matter of convenience each geographic elder is assigned members in a geographic zone and then becomes the elder for these parishioners. Such geographic boundaries may change from time to time but no congregational member will be without an elder assigned. The chairman may act as an elder to new members for a period of time (less than six months) until their assignment/transfer to a geographic elder.

    Pending voters assembly approval, up to three "special needs" elders could be added to the Board of Elders by the Board itself. These "special needs" elders would not have geographic zones assigned them, but in every other respect would have full membership on the Board of Elders (one elder = one vote) and full responsibility.

5. The Board of Elders shall serve as special assistants to the pastor(s), supporting them with prayer, helping them with special problems in their ministry, and concerning itself with the spiritual, emotional and physical health and welfare of the pastor(s) and their families. It shall ensure that they are provided with adequate compensation, housing, and assistance with their work to guarantee them sufficient free time for personal responsibilities, study and relaxation.

6. The Board of Elders shall help the pastor(s) cultivate a spirit of harmony among the congregation members.

7. The Board of Elders shall be responsible for providing the pastor(s) with adequate pulpit and altar assistance.

8. The Board of Elders shall arrange for pastoral services when a vacancy occurs in the office, including the exercising of proper leadership in calling a pastor. No less than one elder shall be included on any call committee. The chairman can be assigned and count toward this minimum representation.

Pastor Needs

9. The Board of Elders shall be responsible for the proper conduct of public congregational worship services.

10. The Board of Elders shall make appropriate recommendations to the church council regarding the reception of new members, peaceful release and the transfer of members.

11. The Board of Elders shall on rare occasion need to become involved in the spiritual welfare and activities of the preschool and day school run by the congregation, particularly under such circumstances where a potential exists for the spiritual welfare of the congregation to be harmed in any way. The day school and preschool are considered to be part of the congregation.

12. The Board of Elders shall appoint a worship committee to consist of: a pastor, minister of music of the congregation, an elder and a minimum of three baptized members, one of whom shall be appointed as chairman, to make recommendations regarding the public worship services of the congregation. All segments of the congregation should be considered if and when recommended changes are contemplated.

13. The Board of Elders shall appoint a committee on ushering to consist of a head usher and two assistants, plus at least two advisors from past (experienced) serving ushers.

14. The Board of Elders shall appoint a social ministry committee to consist of a chairman and others as "helping hands" in Jesus' name to extend to fellow souls in need.

15. The Board of Elders shall appoint a new members committee that shall consist of a chairman and others to assist in the assimilation of new members into the congregation.

—From "LCMS Job Descriptions: Congregation Officer: Elders," *pp. 6–7.* The Lutheran Church—Missouri Synod, *http://www.lcms.org/Document.fdoc?src=lcm&id=1196.*

NOTES

CHAPTER 1

1. *Wisdom for Pastors Seeking Joy in Their Ministry*, John W. Kleinig (Doxology, Inc., 2009), DVD.
2. "The Role of Elders," *LCMS FAQ: Worship/Congregational Life*. The Lutheran Church—Missouri Synod, www.lcms.org/Document. fdoc?src=lcm&id=545 (October 2011).
3. Commission on Theology and Church Relations of The Lutheran Church—Missouri Synod, *A Brief Statement of the Doctrinal Position of the Missouri Synod: Of the Public Ministry* [Adopted 1932] (St. Louis: Concordia, N.D.), http://www.iclnet.org/pub/resources/text/ wittenberg/mosynod/web/doct-12.html.
4. Dietrich Bonhoeffer, *Dietrich Bonhoeffer's Christmas Sermons* (Grand Rapids: Zondervan, 2005), 80.
5. Eugene H. Peterson, *The Contemplative Pastor: Returning to the Art of Spiritual Direction* (Grand Rapids: Eerdmans, 1989), 138–39.

CHAPTER 2

1. Victor A. Constien, *The Caring Elder: A Training Manuel for Serving* (St. Louis: Concordia, 1986), 24–25.
2. Armin W. Schuetze and Irwin J. Habeck, *The Shepherd under Christ* (Milwaukee: Northwestern, 1974), 90.
3. Arthur J. Clement, *The Shepherd's Assistants: A Handbook for Church Elders or Deacons* (Milwaukee: Northwestern, 2007), 20.
4. Johann Gerhard, *Meditations on Divine Mercy* (St. Louis: Concordia, 2003), 43.
5. *Lutheran Service Book* (St. Louis: Concordia, 2006), 151.
6. Clement, *The Shepherd's Assistants*, 20.
7. Hermann Sasse, "The Crisis of the Christian Ministry," in *The Lonely Way: Selected Essays and Letters,* translated by Matthew C. Harrison, et al. (St. Louis: Concordia, 2002), 2:371–72.

Chapter 3

1. Talent Smart, "Emotional Intelligence Appraisal," http://talentsmart .com (October 2010).

Chapter 4

1. Dale A. Meyer, "Loose Ends and Ragged Edges," *Concordia Journal* 36, no. 4 (Fall 2010): 315.
2. Meyer, "Loose Ends," 315–16.
3. John W. Kleinig, *Grace upon Grace: Spirituality for Today* (St. Louis: Concordia, 2008), 100.
4. Michael Horton, *Christless Christianity: The Alternative Gospel of the American Church* (Grand Rapids: Baker Books, 2009), 16–17.
5. Horton, *Christless Christianity*, 18.

Chapter 5

1. Gene Edward Veith Jr., *God at Work: Your Christian Vocation in All of Life* (Wheaton, IL: Crossway, 2002), 52–53.
2. Veith, *God at Work*, 40.
3. Gene Edward Veith Jr., *The Spirituality of the Cross: The Way of the First Evangelicals*, rev. ed. (St. Louis: Concordia, 2010), 104–5.
4. Paul T. McCain, gen. ed., *Concordia: The Lutheran Confessions*, 2nd ed. (St. Louis: Concordia, 2005, 2006), 41.
5. Os Guinness, *Dining with the Devil: The Megachurch Movement Flirts with Modernity* (Grand Rapids: Hourglass Books, 1993), 39.

Chapter 6

1. Peter C. Bender, "The Ordination of a Minister," in *Lutheran Catechesis: Catechuman Edition,* 2nd ed. (Sussex, WI: The Concordia Catechetical Academy), 139–40. Copyright © 2008 Concordia Catechetical Academy. Used with permission. All rights reserved.
2. What is not considered in such a thought process is that when someone is unrepentant in regard to their sin, they've already left!